EARTH
WILL SURVIVE*

*but we may not

Katie Coppens

For further information, contact:
Tumblehome, Inc.
201 Newbury St, Suite 201
Boston, MA 02116
https://tumblehomebooks.org/

Library of Congress Control Number: 2021941429
hardcover
ISBN 13: 978-1-943431-73-1
ISBN 10: 1-943431-73-6
paperback
ISBN 13: 978-1-943431-77-9
ISBN 10: 1-943431-77-9

Coppens, Katie / Earth Will Survive / Katie Coppens
— 1st ed

Cover Design: Katie Coppens
Book Design: Yu-Yi Ling

Printed in Taiwan
10 9 8 7 6 5 4 3 2 1

Tumblehome, Inc.

EARTH
WILL SURVIVE*
*but we may not

A history of humans' understanding of
Earth, our impact on it, and the steps
we must take to save countless species—
including our own.

This book is dedicated to the *we* in the book's title:

The *we* includes all species on Earth, from the
boulder star coral to the African baobab tree
to the lemur leaf frog to the snow leopard
to the green sea turtle to the pink pimelea
to the moss mite to the rusty patched bumblebee
to the mountain gorilla to the gray bat
to the European hamster to the Lear's macaw
to the blue whale to the human.

For when it comes to the climate crisis,
we're all endangered.

Part 3

Actions Speak Louder than Words:
How You Can Help

Part 4

In Conclusion: We have a Choice

Glossary

To Further Your Understanding

Acknowledgments

About The Author

Sources

Photo Credits

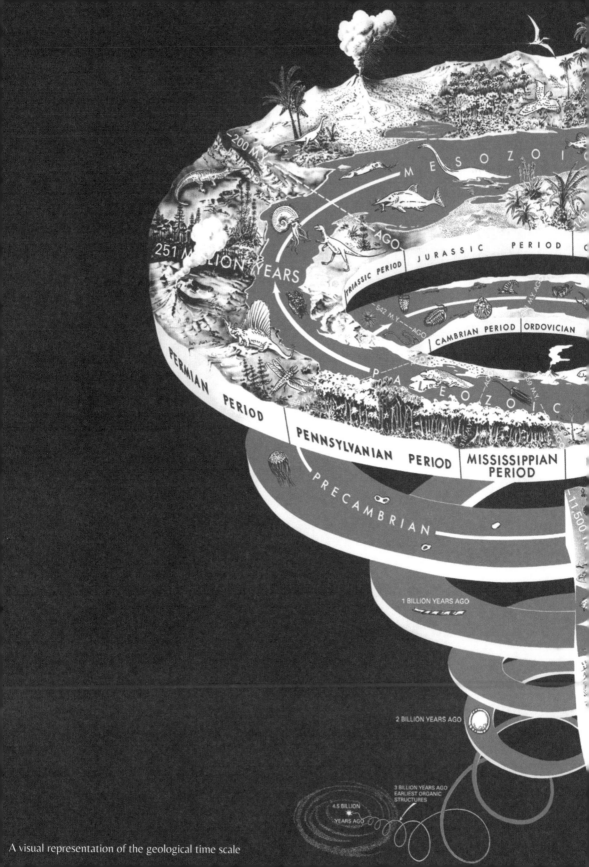

A visual representation of the geological time scale

E arth's story is a long one; it's over 4,543,000,000 years old. Earth is one planet among 100 billion planets in just our galaxy. And our galaxy is one galaxy out of an estimated two trillion galaxies. We don't know how unique our planet is out of the estimated 700,000,000,000,000,000,000,000 planets in the Universe, but we do know how special it is to us. Earth is our home. And in many ways, it's also our teacher.

Earth teaches us about its past through rocks, ice cores, and fossils. From Earth's evidence and humans' scientific understanding, we've learned that Earth began when particles of cosmic gas and dust compressed. The varying density of Earth's elements caused layers to form. Earth's inner core is mostly made of solid iron and is the hottest, densest part of Earth. The following layer is the outer core, which is mostly iron and nickel in a liquid form. Next is the mantle, which makes up most of Earth's volume; it has rock that gets so hot that it flows. This flowing rock is called magma, which moves at about the same rate that human fingernails grow. Convection currents in the mantle cause Earth's tectonic plates to move, which cause earthquakes and mountains to form. Earth's surface is called the crust, which is where all of Earth's species have lived.

As Earth cooled, it sweated out gases and steam, which would become Earth's atmosphere. This atmosphere allowed the build-up of water vapor, which condensed and rained down, filling Earth's oceans. About three to three and a half billion years ago, the first life, in the form of single-celled microorganisms, began on Earth. The first bacteria were anaerobic, which means they didn't require oxygen for respiration. Over time, life evolved, photosynthesis began, and the "Great Oxidation Event" occurred, which led to an accumulation of oxygen in the atmosphere. More oxygen led to more species. Plant and animal life slowly evolved and became more complex. More algae developed, followed by jellyfish and trilobites. Over time, some plants evolved to live on land, and some animals evolved in movement by developing backbones.

Everything on Earth has slowly changed over time, even

the continents; at one time the continents were together in one supercontinent—*Pangaea*. Tectonic plates have grinded, shifted, pushed together, and pulled apart, causing the continents to move and reshape, again and again. Earth currently has seven continents with biomes ranging from tundra to desert to tropical rainforest. Deep and diverse oceans separate the continents; some regions have floating icebergs while others have brightly colored coral reefs.

The species of plants and animals on Earth are as varied as their habitats. Like Earth's land and water, its species have changed again and again. Earth's rocks build up in layers, with new layers of rock forming on top of older rock layers. Rocks hold fossils, which are the remains or imprints of organisms. And fossils hold the stories of Earth's past. Since life began on Earth, new species have developed. Some of these species have survived, while some have gone extinct. Fossils reveal that extinction can occur slowly over generations or quickly due to catastrophic events.

The biggest life-ending event that changed Earth's atmosphere, oceans, habitats, and species occurred 248 million years ago and is known as "the great dying." Atmospheric changes from thousands of years of volcanic eruptions caused oceans to warm and become acidic. As a result, over 90% of Earth's species went extinct. "The great dying" is one of five mass extinctions from Earth's past, known as the "Big Five." The species that survived reproduced again and again, and evolved over time, until new species dominated Earth.

A few million years after "The Great Dying," dinosaurs, a

group of reptiles that came in all shapes and sizes, evolved. Like so many species before, dinosaurs also suffered a mass extinction. Sixty-six million years ago, Earth experienced its most dramatic day, leaving it with one of its most significant scars—the Chicxulub crater. On this day, a six-mile wide asteroid crashed into Earth traveling at 12 miles per second! Creatures that lived as far as two thousand miles away were vaporized within minutes of the asteroid's impact. Debris and ash clogged Earth's atmosphere and blocked out much of the Sun's light. Of Earth's species, 75% went extinct, including the land dinosaurs, nearly all bird-like dinosaurs, and 90% of all mammals.

Like previous extinctions, this one created opportunities for the surviving insects, birds, reptiles, and mammals. Many of the mammals that survived lived below ground, and they were all smaller than the size of a modern-day cat. These small mammals had previously been a food source for larger species and now benefited in the aftermath of the asteroid's impact because they needed less food to survive than their larger neighbors. These mammals went on to take various evolutionary routes, one of which led to primates.

Over time, primates also evolved in various ways. One of the ways would eventually lead along the branch of hominins to *Homo sapiens*... our species. Some scientists believe that around 6 million years ago, one of the early hominins began to walk upright. Our ancestors then evolved and changed in many ways, from the shape of their feet to the size of their brains. Our species, *Homo sapiens*, emerged around 200,000 years ago. Then, around 12,000 years ago, people began farming. With more food available, cities began to form—and with them, civilizations.

Humans have chosen the names for all known extinct and living species on Earth, including ourselves. *Homo sapiens* means "wise man" in Latin. *Homo sapiens* is but one species out of an estimated 8,700,000 species currently on Earth. *Homo sapiens* has the intelligence to study the past, record the present, and make predictions for the future. We have the technology to explore distant galaxies and study Earth's tiniest organisms. We can communicate across our planet in a moment. We can examine evidence and decide which path is the wisest to take. We can learn from one another and make a plan to change our actions.

We are an advanced species, yet we don't always choose to listen to the story that Earth is telling us. Earth doesn't just teach us about its past, it also teaches us about the present. Earth speaks through its melting glaciers and rising oceans, carbon dioxide levels and ocean acidification, and the extinction of species. Earth's evidence shows us that our species, *Homo sapiens*, is changing Earth faster than it can keep up. Our species, *Homo sapiens*, is changing Earth faster than *we* can keep up.

Yet, as a species, we are divided. Some choose to believe the evidence of Earth's current climate change, while some choose to ignore or, even worse, deny it and call it a "hoax." Climate change is happening, and it's killing species at a rate that we haven't seen since that six-mile wide asteroid hit 66 million years ago. Looking at evidence of climate change and discussing possible solutions should not divide us as a species. Instead, saving Earth's habitats and species should be the most unifying cause that humans have ever faced. No species in the past have had the ability to understand the signs or consequences of their actions. The nature of who we are as a species, as *Homo sapiens*, has led us into our current climate crisis, but it's also what could save us from it.

For, if we don't make changes now, the reality is that Earth will survive, but we may not.

Part 1

Background:
Homo Sapiens' Understanding of Earth's History

Our understanding
of Earth's history has built up
much like rocks do... slowly over time.

Chapter 1

Curiosities

Before examining *Homo sapiens*' impact on Earth, we'll first explore our species' understanding of Earth and how this understanding has changed over time. Part one of this book includes many of the most significant theories and discoveries about Earth's history over the past 400 years. With each new realization, not only did our perceptions of Earth change, but so did our understanding of our own species. The knowledge from part one of the book will serve as the foundation for the evidence about our current climate crises, which will be explained in part two. In part three, you'll learn steps you can take to create positive change.

Let's start by imagining that you discover a dinosaur bone. Only, you don't know that it's a dinosaur bone because you don't know that there once were dinosaurs. You see part of a bone poking out of the ground, then dig and dig and dig until all six feet of the bone are revealed. The bone's

Dinosaur Bone (femur)

shape leads you to believe that it's a femur, which is the upper portion of an animal's leg. How could there be a six-foot-long leg bone? What could it have come from?

Now imagine that someone told you that it was the leg bone from an enormous reptile, a sauropod dinosaur, with a neck and tail that stretched 115 feet in length! And it was 40 feet tall *and* weighed 175,000 pounds. What would your reaction be? If you're like most people, you'd be skeptical that this could be true. If you're like some people, you'd do everything you could to claim this concept was a "hoax" and publicly criticize the person saying it. Throughout history, people have been reluctant to acknowledge scientific discovery because it has caused them to question what they believed to be true.

One example of this reluctance concerns extinct species. Throughout most of human history, people didn't know that species could go extinct. There was no understanding of a world where animals looked different in the past, nor the possibility that some species could survive (and evolve) while others died out. Moreover, people thought that humans were the center of the Universe. This belief is important to keep in mind throughout this chapter because much of human history was shaped by misconceptions about Earth and *Homo sapiens*' role on Earth.

sauropod dinosaur remains

The leading voice throughout much of civilized time came from religious theory about the origins of Earth. As a result, when discoveries were made, like a very long femur bone, they were labeled as "curiosities." These curiosities are now what we understand to be prehistoric fossils. The journey for humans to fully understand the historical and scientific value of fossils took centuries to unfold.

Archbishop James Usher

Much of the reason it took so long is due to inaccurate understandings of Earth's age. In 1654, Archbishop James Usher (1581-1656) used his interpretation of the Bible to estimate that Earth was around 5,650 years old. In actuality, Usher's estimate was off by over four and a half billion years. Usher was a well-respected religious figure, and as a result, his estimate that Earth formed on October 23, 4004 BCE held sway for hundreds of years.

As more and more "curiosities" were found in the 1700s, people asked more questions. One set of challenging finds were mastodons, which were slightly smaller than today's elephants. Like elephants, they were herbivores that grazed and traveled in herds. Because mastodons went extinct only around 10,000 years ago, their remains are near Earth's surface. In 1739, elephant-like remains were found in what is now the location of Big Bone Lick State Park in Kentucky. Native Americans traveling with French troops were hunting in a marsh near the Ohio River when they found a tooth that weighed ten pounds, along with large thigh bones and tusks, in the mud. The remains were sent to Louis XV, the King of France, where they were put in a museum. The bones were surrounded by controversy because of where they were found, far from the elephants of African and Asia,

Mastodon remains

and because although they looked like elephant remains, they showed slight differences.

Think back to that dinosaur bone found before people knew species could go extinct. Now imagine people finding teeth similar to elephant teeth, yet slightly different, in locations where elephants don't currently live. How could this be explained? Many people relied on the biblical story of Noah's Ark and the Great Flood to explain the existence of any "curiosities." In the Genesis story, Noah saved his family and a male and female of each animal by building a giant ark to keep them safe as it rained for 40 days. During this massive flood, people reasoned, drowned animals could be swept away, even across oceans. People used this biblical story to explain how remains that resembled certain animals, such as those they believed came from an elephant, could turn up far from where those animals live in the present day.

In 1795, James Hutton (1726-1797), who would later be called the "father of geology," questioned Usher's long-standing claim of Earth's age. Hutton was a Scottish land-owner and a gentleman farmer, which means he owned a farm as part of his estate, but farmed more for joy than profit. He wrote a book called *Theory of Earth, with Proofs and Illustrations* from years of studying the soil, erosion, deposition, and rock layers. This book explained many aspects of the rock cycle that we know today, including how rocks weather and build up over time. Rather than a biblical explanation for sedimentary rocks forming from the floods of Noah's Ark, Hutton believed that as sand and mud were deposited over time, until they eventually formed sedimentary rock. Hutton emphasized observation, evidence, and the importance of a scientific approach. Many disregarded Hutton's theories because he did not use the Bible as a source of evidence and opposed Usher's belief that Earth was only a few thousand years old.

James Hutton

However, Hutton's explanations set the groundwork for Georges Cuvier (1769-1832), who gave an explanation for the "curiosities" found around the world. Cuvier, a Frenchman, introduced the world to a new term, *espèces perdues* or

lost species, which we now call extinct species. Georges Cuvier studied controversial remains, including elephant-like bones that were found in Siberia, another land region that doesn't have modern-day elephants. In 1796, during a public lecture, he explained his belief that unidentifiable remains were from species that no longer exist. Like Hutton, Cuvier based his arguments on scientific observation and inferences, and like Hutton's, his claims were considered blasphemy—speech against religion.

Georges Cuvier

Many continued to argue that "curiosities" were the bones from animals washing ashore during the biblical flood. People also argued that to suggest that species could go extinct was to speak against the perfection of God's divine creation. Beliefs or theories that could be interpreted as anti-religious were disregarded, and often the person making (or defending) them was criticized. But despite the negative reactions to Cuvier, more and more unidentifiable remains continued to be found. By 1812, Cuvier identified 49 different "lost species."

In 1811, in the British seaside town of Lyme Regis in Dorset, twelve-year-old Mary Anning (1799-1847) and her older brother Joseph (1796-1849) excavated a four-foot-long skull in a cliff. They believed the skull could be from a crocodile. The skull and 60 vertebrae would later be identified as

Mary Anning

forming part of an ichthyosaur, a large extinct marine reptile that lived from 250 to 90 million years ago. This was a time when women did not yet have the right to vote in England—and wouldn't get that right for over 100 years—so you can imagine how many educated men disregarded Anning's discovery simply because she was a woman, let alone a poor woman without a science background. Mary Anning continued to discover fossils that drew public attention.

In 1824, now in her mid-twenties, Mary Anning excavated the first full plesiosaur. Georges Cuvier heard of her discovery and initially declared it to be a fake because of the length of the creature's neck in proportion to its body. After seeing the fossil in person, Cuvier admitted he was wrong and authenticated it himself, confirming it to be the remains of an extinct marine reptile. With Cuvier's verification of her work, Mary Anning became one of the world's most famous fossil hunters. Her discoveries included the first complete Dimorphodon fossil and the first remains of a pterosaur found in the British Isles. Mary Anning's landmark discoveries and Georges Cuvier's explanation of extinction changed our understanding of prehistoric creatures and the stories that their fossils tell of Earth's past.

Mary Anning's Plesiosaur

Yet, it's important to know that the information that fossils give us is incomplete because so many fossils have yet to be discovered or are too ill-preserved to ever be discovered. Currently, it's estimated that 15% of living species on Earth have been catalogued, with countless unknown species in categories like insects and fungi. In the oceans, it's estimated that only 10% of ocean organisms have been identified. If such a small percentage of *living* species have been catalogued, imagine how many species from Earth's past are unknown. One of the greatest challenges is that older fossils, particularly before the Cambrian Period, are rare. Deep-lying fossils are harder to find and are more likely to be damaged due to rocks building up over time. Older, and therefore deeper, rocks are also more likely to change due to heat and pressure, which can destroy fossils.

Also, earlier life was less complex; without hard remains, specimens were less likely to be preserved as fossils.

Current scientific understanding has come, and will continue to come, from Earth's rock layers and the fossils that have been discovered. In the 19th century, using fossils and the understanding that rocks build up from the oldest on the bottom to the most recent on top, which is called the *law of superposition*, geologists concluded that Earth was closer to 100 million years old. Today, the age of fossils is determined by measuring radioactive decay. Elements which are commonly used in radiometric dating include uranium, potassium, and carbon which decay into lead, argon, and nitrogen. Zircon crystals, which can be a tenth of a millimeter long and contain small amounts of uranium and thorium, are also used to date when rocks formed. Radiometric dating has led to a current estimate of Earth being 4,543,000,000 years old.

Through centuries of scientific discovery, our estimate of Earth's age has increased by over four and a half billion years. Today, we live with a much more accurate sense of Earth and its place in the Universe. Yet, we often forget that what are now widely accepted facts were first discovered, questioned, scrutinized, and often dismissed before they were eventually understood.

Chapter 2

The Evolution of Evolution

One of the bravest things you can do is be willing to question what others believe to be true. As a species, our understanding of the world continues to evolve and change, much as Earth and its species have evolved and changed.

Maria Sibylla Merian (1647-1717) was a naturalist and a scientific illustrator who published her first book in 1675. With this and other publications, she became one of the

Maria Sibylla Merian

leading entomologists of her time. Of course, in her time, the word entomologist didn't yet exist—it wouldn't be used until 1764—but she was known as someone who studied insects. Her drawings of insects and documentation of the metamorphosis of butterflies led to more studies of these creatures and helped break the widespread belief that bugs were "beasts of the devil." Her drawings also helped Swedish naturalist Carl Linnaeus, who lived from 1707 to 1778, identify an estimated 100 new species.

Carl Linnaeus, who would be called the "father of taxonomy," went on to identify thousands of plant and animal species. Linnaeus died when Georges Cuvier was just a boy, yet in many ways Linnaeus added to the skepticism around fossils. People began to sell "curiosities" for money, and sometimes it could be difficult to recognize when curiosities (what we now call fossils) were fake. One example of a fake fossil that Linnaeus unmasked was a mythical hydra—a seven-headed snake, which the Mayor of Hamburg claimed to own. Upon examination, Linnaeus revealed that the

Carl Linnaeus

bones were from the remains of weasels and snakes joined together. To make it easier to spot a fake fossil, Linnaeus started to group similar organisms. Linnaeus went on to create a classification system for organisms based on shared physical characteristics, which has been modified over time to include: domain, kingdom, phylum, class, order, family genus, and species.

With both curiosity and suspicion growing in regards to fossils, as we saw with Mary Anning's discovery of the Plesiosaur, the 1800s were a time of differing thoughts about the concept that animals could go extinct. Much skepticism around Cuvier's *lost species* came from his inability to explain why some species went extinct and how other new species could emerge.

Charles Lyell

In 1830, Charles Lyell (1797-1875) published a book called *Principles of Geology* in which he explained that Earth continuously changes, but that "the present is key to the past"—that is, the same forces that act on the landscape today did so in the past. Two years later, William Whewell would call this concept *uniformitarianism*, which is a founding principle of geology. While Lyell had many correct understandings about geology, he too could not explain why some species went extinct and how new species came to be. He falsely thought that all species could exist at all times.

Meanwhile, on December 27, 1831, Charles Darwin (1809-1882) boarded a ship called HMS *Beagle* and began his five-year journey of discovery. He started the voyage at the age of twenty-two, fresh out of college. The *Beagle* left the United Kingdom and headed to South America.

The ship's purpose was to survey coasts to help make maps more accurate. The voyage continued on from South America to many locations, including New Zealand, Australia, and South Africa. Darwin made countless drawings and collected thousands of specimens of rocks, fossils, plants, and animals throughout this journey. Darwin also read Lyell's three-volume *Principles of Geology* (published between 1830 and 1833).

Charles Darwin

Darwin made his first significant scientific discovery on this journey, which was an observation of how coral reefs form around sinking islands, creating a barrier reef. This discovery helped Darwin meet people in the scientific world, including his role model, Charles Lyell.

When home, Darwin observed and studied all of his specimens together, a task that eventually led to the theory of natural selection. Observations of differing finches Darwin saw on the Galápagos Islands became a key component of this theory. With the collaboration of John Gould (1804-1881), who studied birds, Darwin made his great discovery. He realized that the species of finches from the Galápagos Islands, which are now considered to be fifteen different species called *Darwin's finches*, were all similar, but differed slightly from one another depending on which island they inhabited. They were also different from finches that lived on the mainland of South America. It was believed that the finches came over from the mainland, but the finches on each island varied in their physical features, such as beak shape, feet, and overall size. The differing beaks were evidence of natural selection.

Darwin believed that the beaks differed because the islands had different food sources. For example, the finches that caught insects had long thin beaks, while the finches that needed to crack open nuts had wider beaks. The islands are far enough apart that breeding between islands was unlikely. Therefore, the birds must have changed from the original mainland finches to survive in their habitat. Darwin's theory of natural selection revolves around competition. To explain how these birds may have changed over generations to survive in their habitat, Darwin reflected that some animals are born with natural variations, such as longer beaks. When it came to searching for insects for food, the finches with longer beaks were more likely to survive and reproduce because they could find the food easier and faster in a certain environment. When those birds reproduced and had offspring, their offspring were more likely to have longer beaks, and eventually, over many, many

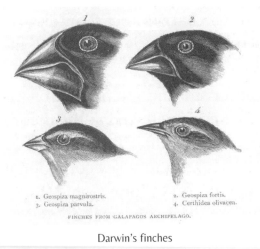

1. Geospiza magnirostris.   2. Geospiza fortis.
3. Geospiza parvula.   4. Certhidea olivacea.

FINCHES FROM GALAPAGOS ARCHIPELAGO.

Darwin's finches

generations, the species changed to all have longer beaks. And it's important to note that other birds whose characteristics were less well adapted for their environment, especially when it was a changing environment, were less likely to survive and reproduce. Darwin came up with the theory of natural selection without knowledge of genetics. Instead the theory was based on observation and inferences.

For almost two decades, Darwin found more evidence, wrote and rewrote his explanation to make sure it was clear. In 1856, Darwin also studied and bred pigeons; he purposely crossed birds with different characteristics to study the offspring. Over this time, he also prepared for the repercussions of a theory that explained species evolving based on competition and survival in their environment. His wife, Emma, was supportive but deeply religious, and this made Darwin mindful of the criticism that he would receive from religious groups. In 1859, at the age of 50, Darwin published *On the Origin of Species.* In the book, Darwin was able to explain both species' extinction and new species' origins. Darwin's theory was so controversial that it ended his friendship with his role model Charles Lyell.

On the Origin of Species

Interestingly, Alfred Russel (A.R.) Wallace (1823-1913), who was twenty years younger than Darwin, was also a British naturalist who made observations based on his travels. In 1848, inspired by naturalists like Darwin, Wallace travelled to the Amazon rainforest with his friend Henry Walter (H.W.) Bates (1825-1892). They travelled together, then parted ways to each focus on their own research. Over four years of travelling via a dugout canoe and fully immersing himself into this habitat, Wallace collected thousands of living and dead specimens. In 1852, on day 26 of his ship's return to England, the ship caught fire and sank with all of his specimens. Ten days later, the passengers and crew were rescued at sea from a passing ship. Wallace spent from 1854-1862 researching in the Malay Archipelago, which is between Southeastern Asia and Australia, collecting over 125,000 specimens, many of which were new scientific discoveries. In 1858, while Wallace was ill and bed bound, he independently came up with the concept of evolution through natural selection. Wallace knew about Darwin's specimens and his work, so Wallace wrote to him outlining the details of his discovery. Darwin presented his own writings on the topic as well as Wallace's to the Linnean Society (named after Carl Linnaeus). Many believe it was the awareness that Wallace was developing evidence for a similar theory that propelled Darwin to finally outline his theory in a book in 1859. With Darwin's writing of *On the Origin of Species,* he became known as "the

A.R. Wallace

father of evolution."

More evidence for Darwin's theory arose from Henry Walter Bates' Amazon specimens, which he sent home on three different ships so they would not have the same fate as Wallace's. In 1861, Bates published examples of butterflies using mimicry, in which butterflies imitate other species, as a method of survival. A few years later, in 1866, an understanding of genetics came from Gregor Mendel (1822-1884). Mendel was an Austrian monk who is known as the "father of modern genetics." Mendel raised

and cross-pollinated pea plants to show how traits like flower color and plant height passed down through generations. Eventually, Mendel's work led to an understanding of dominant and recessive traits and hereditary mutations. Together, these concepts helped explain how new traits can be genetically passed onto offspring. The long thin beak of the seed-seeking finch was a trait that helped it survive; there-

Gregor Mendel

fore, since offspring inherit traits from parents, a long thin beak was more likely to make its way into lots of offspring. Over time, natural selection would determine how species changed and which species died.

For over 150 years, Charles Darwin's theory has stirred up strong emotions, especially in regard to human evolution. In 1758, Carl Linnaeus introduced the species name of *Homo sapiens.* Humans are now believed to be one mammal out of over 6,000 mammals on Earth, and one animal out of 1.6 million species we've identified—with an estimate that there may be as many as 8.7 million species on Earth. Yet since the realization that humans are a type of animal, some people have focused on the differences between humans and other animals, while others have focused on the similarities.

Those who focus on the similarities know that all living species are related. All species have origins in the Earth's first single-celled organisms. There is variety to Earth's species of today and the past because species have taken various evolutionary paths. As Darwin found, organisms pass on traits to their offspring and these traits determine if organisms, and on a bigger scale, species live or die. Habitats changing—quickly and slowly—has been the cause of countless extinctions. And these extinctions have impacted the evolutionary journey of all of today's species, including *Homo sapiens.* The six-mile wide asteroid that slammed into Earth 66 million years ago resulted in the demise of 75% of our planet's species. This mass extinction event caused the death of the land dinosaurs and created significant evolutionary opportunities for mammals.

Mammals evolved in many different directions, and the first primates are believed to have lived around 56 million years ago. *Homo sapiens* are primates. Primates are split into two suborders, either Strepsirrhini—which are defined by their wet noses, such as lemurs—or Haplorhini—which are defined by their dry noses, such as apes. Humans are

Haplorhini, which we can subdivide even farther until we get to our tribe, the hominins, which also includes chimpanzees.

Some scientists believe that around six million years ago, one of the early hominins began to walk upright. Our ancestors then evolved and changed in many ways. There were various hominins, including *Homo neanderthalensis* (the Neanderthals), *Homo erectus, Homo habilis,* and various species of *Australopithecus.* Our species, *Homo sapiens,* emerged around 200 thousand years ago. We can determine how closely related two species are by comparing their DNA, the genetic code for organisms. That's how we have learned that our current closest relatives in the animal kingdom include gorillas and chimpanzees. In fact, *Homo sapiens'* and chimpanzees' DNA are 98.8% the same. Our species' evolution has gone beyond biological and

Representations of
Homo sapiens

genetic changes to include using tools, farming, and forming civilizations.

For much of civilized history, our understanding of Earth was incorrect. Earth's great age and the realities of extinction and evolution were, understandably, challenging concepts for many people to accept. They are still challenging for some today. This chapter began by saying that one of the bravest things you can do is be willing to question what others believe to be true. Yes, but what is even braver is to be willing to question what *you* believe to be true.

A chimpanzee

Chapter 3

An Outsider's Insight

Being a scientist requires both a critical eye and bold heart. The scientific method involves data collection and conclusions, yet it also involves a willingness to take a risk and question what is assumed to be true. Sometimes, the unconventional perspective of an outsider can challenge long-standing interpretations of the world. Historically, and sometimes even today, people are dismissed as unqualified outsiders due to their gender, age, nationality, or education. Still, it was often these outsiders' unique perspective that allowed them to see what others did not.

One such person is Alfred Wegener (1880-1930), a German meteorologist with a degree in astronomy. His study of polar climates took him on four expeditions to Greenland, which is within the Arctic Circle. Some of his research included observing weather from a hot air balloon. On one trip, in 1906, he and his brother Kurt broke the world record for an uninterrupted hot air balloon flight of 52 hours.

Alfred Wegener

From his vantage point in the sky, Wegener noticed how pieces of ice broke apart and moved. This discovery, in connection with his observation of world maps and seeing how the shape of the continents, such as the eastern coast of South America and the northwestern coast of Africa, match up like puzzle pieces, led him to believe that at one time there was a supercontinent. Wegener named this supercontinent *Pangaea*, which means "all lands" in Ancient Greek. Wegener published his first paper on this theory in 1915, stating, "The continents must have shifted. South America must have lain alongside Africa and formed a unified block... The two parts must then have become increasingly separated over a period of millions of years like pieces of a cracked ice floe in water."

Fossils are a link between geology and biology. A major piece of evidence for Wegener's theory of continental

Part 1

drift was fossils of various plant and animal species that matched up across continents. For example, the *Mesosaurus*, an extinct reptile that was about three feet long, lived from 299 to 271 million years ago. There are Mesosaurus fossil remains in the eastern part of South America and the western part of Africa that line up when fitted together. These continents are thousands of miles apart, which would have been too far for the Mesosaurus to swim; therefore, these fossil remains serve as evidence for Wegener's theory that the continents were once joined.

Wegener was not a geologist. As a result, he was viewed as an outsider, and geologists, with international criticism, rejected his theory of continental drift. In regards to Wegener's fossil evidence, many geologists (falsely) believed that fossils, such as the Mesosaurus, matched up across Africa and South America because of a land bridge across the Atlantic Ocean. They believed this land bridge sank into the ocean over time. Moreover, it was easy to criticize Wegener's theory because he could not explain what caused the continents to move.

Wegener died in 1930 while on a research trip to Greenland. One year after his death, in 1931, Arthur Holmes (1890-1965), the author of *The Age of Earth*, published a paper that suggested that Earth's heat caused convection currents in the mantle, which caused the continents to move. Holmes would later be known as the "father of the geologic time scale", but even with this publication, it took decades for Wegener's theory that the continents have changed location to receive wide support.

Bruce Heezen and Marie Tharp's research from 1946 to 1952 provided evidence for Wegener's theory. Bruce Heezen (1924-1977), a geologist, collected data from ships by

Marie Tharp and Bruce Heezen

using sound to measure depth. Marie Tharp (1920-2006) interpreted this data to make the Atlantic Ocean's first detailed map, including all of its underwater mountains and valleys. In the process, they mapped the Mid-Atlantic Ridge, which is a location of seafloor spreading. In 1962, Harry Hammond Hess (1906-1969) published "The History of Ocean Basins." Hess's writing explained seafloor spreading, which occurs when convection currents cause Earth's tectonic plates to split apart and new rock to form. The work by Holmes, Hess, Heezen, Tharp, and other scientists eventually led to an understanding of plate tectonics. And plate tectonics supplied evidence for Wegener's theory of continental drift.

Another example of an outsider with insight was Rachel Carson (1907-1964). She was a biologist and the author of award-winning nonfiction books, such as *Under the Sea-Wind, The Sea Around Us,* and *The Edge of the Sea.* Carson studied pesticides when working for the U.S. Bureau of

Rachel Carson

Fisheries. A major insecticide of her time was DDT, dichlorodiphenyltrichloroethane. Developed in the 1940s, DDT was sprayed widely to protect people from insect-spread diseases such as malaria, as well as on crops to kill insects. In 1958, Carson received a letter from her friend Olga Owens Huckins (1900-1968) who described birds dying on her two-acre bird sanctuary after planes sprayed DDT. Rachel Carson then spent four years researching the impact of DDT and its consequences on species and the environment. In an interview, Carson said, "These sprays, dusts, and aerosols are now applied almost universally to farms, gardens, forests, and homes. Nonselective chemicals that have the power to kill every insect—the good and the bad—to still the song of birds and the leaping of fish in the streams. All this though the intended target may be only a few weeds or insects." Many negative impacts were found on how the pesticide's toxins traveled through the food chain. Carson even found an effect on the eggs of birds. The toxins caused bird shells to become too thin for baby birds to survive, which led to dramatic population decreases. Imagining a world without birdsong led Rachel Carson to title her 1962 book *Silent Spring,* which exposed the dangers of chemical pesticides.

Rachel Carson should not have been viewed as an outsider, but the pesticide industry did everything it could to discredit her. A spokesman for the chemical industry, Dr. Robert White Stevens, stated in an interview that was shown nationwide that, "The major claims in Miss Rachel Carson's book *Silent Spring* are gross distortions of the actual facts, completely unsupported by scientific experimental evidence and general practical experience in the field. If man were to faithfully follow the teachings of Miss Carson, we would return to the dark ages and the insects, and diseases, vermin would once again inherit the earth." He added, "Miss Carson maintains that the balance of nature is a major force in the survival of man, whereas the modern chemist, the modern biologist, the modern scientist believes that man is steadily controlling nature."

Rachel Carson's book led to public outcry, and within a decade, most DDT uses in the United States had been prohibited. Restrictions around the use of DDT led to increases in many bird populations. One bird that benefitted is America's national symbol, the bald eagle. The U.S. Fish and Wildlife Service reported that in 1963 there were 487 pairs of bald eagles in the continental United States. In 1972, DDT was banned in the United States, and by 1974, the

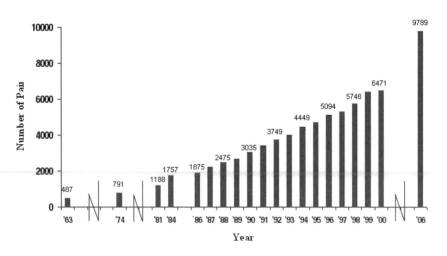

Bald eagle breeding pairs from 1963-2006 in the lower 48 states

number of pairs rose to 791. In 1981, there were 1,188 pairs, and in 2000, there were 6,471 pairs. In 2007, the bald eagle was taken off the list of threatened and endangered species in the United States.

Walter and Luis Alvarez were also viewed as outsiders for their theory that land dinosaurs went extinct as a result of an asteroid hitting Earth. In 1977, Walter Alvarez (1940-), a geologist, was in Italy studying paleomagnetism—an extension of Hess's starting work on plate tectonics. Alvarez examined a rock layer in Gubbio, which is known for showing Earth's long geological record. When Alvarez studied it, he found something unexpected. In one

Luis and Walter Alvarez in Gubbio, Italy

layer of clay, there were no forams, which are single-celled organisms that have shells and live in the ocean. Walter showed this evidence to his father Luis Alvarez (1911-1988), a physics professor at the University of California, Berkeley, and the winner of the Nobel Prize in Physics in 1968.

Colleagues of theirs at Berkeley, Frank Asaro (1927-2014) and Helen Vaughn Michel (1932-), who were chemists, helped them date the clay sample using the element iridium, of which there were unusually high amounts. The group found that the layer dated to the same time that the dinosaurs went extinct and that the high levels of iridium were also found

Helen Vaughn Michel, Frank Asaro, Walter Alvarez, and Luis Alvarez

at that same rock layer at different locations around the world. The layer had an iridium concentration of 6.3 parts per billion, where iridium is typically closer to 0.3 parts per billion in the Earth's crust. They also knew that meteorites have high levels of iridium. This evidence led them to believe that Earth must have been struck by a meteorite that vaporized, leaving iridium to fall all over the Earth. Any meteor that large was certainly large enough to cause death for countless organisms, including the dinosaurs.

Despite the evidence, the asteroid-impact theory was widely disregarded. According to Richard Muller (1944-), a professor of physics at the University of California, Berkeley, and a doctoral student under Luis Alvarez during the time of the Alvarezes' discovery, "Luis Alvarez got very frustrated when the paleontologists didn't say, yes, sir. Thank you for solving our problem. Many of the paleontologists looked on him as someone who didn't know their field and was stepping into this just because it was such a big, important, famous problem."

In 1991, eleven years after the Alvarezes' publication of their theory, the Chicxulub crater, which is not visible from Earth's surface, was discovered and dated to around the time of the hypothesized asteroid's impact. The crater, buried under the Yucatán Peninsula in Mexico, is approximately 100 miles in diameter and twelve miles deep. This was the final piece of evidence that the Alvarezes needed. Today, their asteroid-impact theory is widely believed to be the cause of the mass extinction that occurred 66 million years ago. This mass extinction event serves as another example that shows, as Darwin found, when species have characteristics that are less adapted to a changing environment, they are less likely to survive

Which brings us to our current climate crisis. Someone today who is viewed as an outsider to some people and as a changemaker to others is Greta Thunberg. Born in Sweden in 2003, Thunberg is the world's most recognizable figure bringing awareness and activism to Earth's current climate crisis. In 2018, at the age of fifteen, she won a Swedish newspaper's essay contest in which she wrote about climate change stating, "I want to feel safe. How can I feel safe when I know we are in the greatest crisis in human history?" Rather than going to school, she began protesting outside of the Swedish parliament each Friday with a sign that said "Skolstrejk för klimatet," which translates to *School strike for the climate*. Her protests gained worldwide attention and led to protests by other children and adults. In 2018, Thunberg did a TEDx Talk that has had millions of views, and she addressed the United Nations Climate Change Conference

about the importance of believing the data and science around climate change. In 2019, she spoke at the UN Climate Action Summit with what many call her "How dare you?" speech, in which she challenged the lack of leadership around climate change. In 2019, Thunberg was the youngest person ever to be named Time magazine's "Person of the Year."

Greta Thunberg

   Greta Thunberg cites facts and figures while also questioning why world leaders aren't doing more. She believes that the evidence is clear and there has been too much talk and not enough action. Her use of science without yet having a high school degree, her age, and her direct speaking style are why many criticize her. They look at her as an outsider who does not yet have enough experience to warrant a worldwide audience. Yet, when it comes to climate change and our planet, no one is an outsider. Every living creature has a vested interest in our current climate crisis and what action is taken to help. One of Thunberg's most shared quotes is, "I'd like to tell my grandchildren that we did everything we could. And we did it for them—for the generations to come."

* * * * * *

Earth will survive. Earth has experienced billions of years of change. Extinction and evolution are part of life and why Earth's current species exist today. Yet, one of Earth's species—*Homo sapiens*—is completely unique. We, one species out of millions, have the ability to change Earth's atmosphere, climate and habitats, and to influence which species live and which species die. Humans have much in common with the asteroid that hit Earth 66 million years ago. We are the cause of what many scientists believe to be a current mass extinction event, the sixth mass extinction event in Earth's 4,543,000,000-year history.

The mass extinction event that we are causing is so destructive that even our own species may not survive. A statement like that shouldn't be made without evidence. The next section of this book focuses on the short and long-term evidence of our species' 200,000-year history and how we have impacted other species and caused our planet's current climate crisis. After reading this section, you'll be more educated on our environmental impact and the current climate crisis than most politicians and most people who vote. I want to prepare you that you may get angry reading this section. But, know that understanding the evidence will help us understand the problems and as a result understand the solutions. Throughout this section, there are glimpses of hope through spotlights on people working to help make a difference toward the problems we face. Much like Greta Thunberg, they too are change-makers... they are climate change-makers, they are all working in different ways to change our current climate crisis.

Part 2

Earth Speaks: Evidence of Humans' Impact

Our understanding
of Earth's history has built up
much like rocks do... slowly over time.
Our awareness of our planet, its species,
and humans' impact continues to take shape.
Layers reveal evolving history, science, politics

Chapter 4

Air:

The Critical Balance of Earth's Atmosphere

B reathe in and breathe out. The air you breathe travels from your lungs to your bloodstream. Blood vessels called veins carry blood into your heart while arteries move blood away from your heart. Blood is pumped throughout your body, releasing oxygen to your cells, which make up your tissues and organs. Without Earth's atmosphere and the oxygen it contains, you would no longer be reading this. The atmosphere's delicate balance is an essential factor in why Earth has had life for three and a half billion years.

When Earth first started to form, it was in a hot, molten state—an estimated 3,600° Fahrenheit. It took an estimated

200 million years to cool. As it cooled, gases of hydrogen sulfide, methane, and carbon dioxide sweated out, and volcanoes let out steam filled with hydrogen and oxygen. When Earth's surface cooled to a temperature below boiling, water condensed, rain fell, and oceans formed. Earth's oceans absorb carbon dioxide (CO_2), and this led to an environment in which single-celled organisms could survive. Over time, cyanobacteria evolved and photosynthesis began. Photosynthesis is the process of plants tapping the energy of sunlight to make sugar. In photosynthesis, plants use water, carbon dioxide, and sunlight to manufacture sugar and give off oxygen. With an oxygen-enriched atmosphere, plant and animal life in Earth's oceans continued to evolve.

Marine life expanded rapidly in what we call the *Cambrian explosion*, which occurred from 541 to 530 million years ago. Approximately 100 million years after the Cambrian explosion, the end-Ordovician mass extinction occurred. It's the first of the "big five" mass extinctions and occurred in two pulses between 447 and 443 million years ago. For much of this time, CO_2 levels in the air were approximately fifteen times higher than today, which caused temperatures to increase and sea levels to rise. Earth tends toward balance, and when things get skewed in one direction, other things start to change. One theory is that the plants that colonized land took massive amounts of CO_2 out of the air, causing CO_2 levels to drop dramatically. This led to temperatures dropping so much that Gondwana, Earth's landmass at the time (it would eventually become part of Pangaea), froze. As the air and water get colder, ice forms, causing the sea levels to shrink. Not only do shrinking seas destroy marine ecosystems, but the amount of dissolved oxygen in the water changes. This occurs because cold water holds more oxygen than warm water. Marine organisms have a range of tolerance for dissolved oxygen, and when levels reach beyond that, these organisms will suffocate. During this time, Earth shifted from a "greenhouse" environment to an "icehouse" environment. As a result of the changing habitats, the end-Ordovician mass extinction caused 85% of species to go extinct.

CARBON DIOXIDE OVER 800,000 YEARS

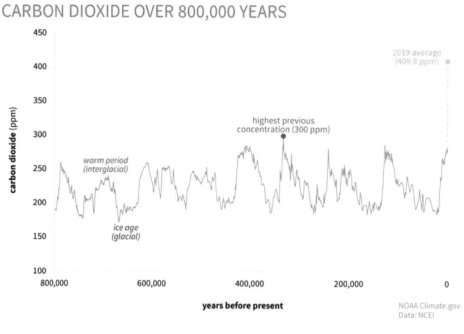

A graph showing CO_2 levels over the past 800,000 years

Just like in the end-Ordovician mass extinction, throughout history Earth's CO_2 levels have fluctuated. Two hundred fifty-two million years ago, massive releases of carbon from volcanoes into the air once again caused temperatures to rise. The End-Permian mass extinction, Earth's largest mass extinction event, has been nicknamed "the great dying." As a result of rising CO_2, the seas warmed by as much as 18°F (10°C). Carbon dioxide caused a highly acidic, greenhouse gas-filled Earth that lasted for an estimated 100,000 to 200,000 years. While most species died, some organisms, such as bacteria, thrived in the hot marine environments. As a result, scientists believe there was so much bacteria in the ocean that it looked purple and was filled with poisonous bubbles. Even the atmosphere was so altered that it's believed the sky looked green. Earth was so toxic and uninhabitable that an estimated 90% of all species went extinct. One of the most well known extinctions from this event are the trilobites, which are now considered an index fossil, a fossil that's so widespread that it's now useful in dating other fossils. Before CO_2 levels increased and the ocean became chemically altered, trilobites had ruled the seas for 270 million years.

This history is important to understand, because many who claim Earth's current climate change is a "hoax" focus on the fact that Earth's climate composition has changed throughout history. Rising and falling CO_2 levels have been the catalyst for mass extinctions; still, the difference between the past and present is that our species, *Homo sapiens*, are causing CO_2 levels and other greenhouse gases to rise at an unprecedented rate. Humans' rising population, consumerism, destruction of forests, and emissions of greenhouse gases from fossil fuels are driving this rapid change.

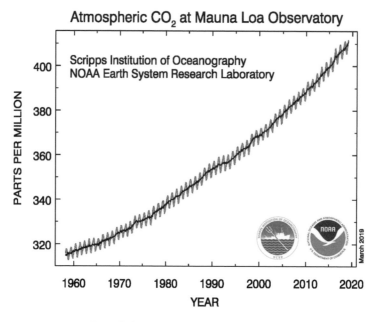

Atmospheric CO$_2$ at Mauna Loa Observatory

Scripps Institution of Oceanography
NOAA Earth System Research Laboratory

PARTS PER MILLION

A graph showing CO$_2$ levels from 1960-2020

Humans' use of fossil fuels can be seen everywhere, from how we travel to where we live to what we buy. Fossil fuels are nonrenewable energy that form from fossilized plants and animals buried deep below the ground. Often these are extracted by drilling or mining, then used as fuel or burned to supply another form of energy such as electricity. It's this burning, whether it happens in a car, a factory, or a power plant, that releases so many emissions into the atmosphere. According to the United States Department of Energy, currently, three-fourths of human emissions come from the burning of fossil fuels. In 2019, fossil fuels added 36.8 billion metric tons of CO$_2$ to the atmosphere. One metric ton is 1,000 kilograms, which is almost 2,204 pounds, now imagine this multiplied by 36,800,000,000.

Fracking, which stands for hydraulic fracturing, has become one of the most divisive topics in the extraction of fossil fuels. When fracking, workers drill as deep as thousands of feet into the ground to reach rock that carries pockets of oil and natural gas. To free those fuels from the rock, the drillers pump in at high pressure a solution called *slick water*. Slick water includes water, acids, and sand or clay that create and then hold open fissures in the rock. This method allows access to fossil fuels that would otherwise be challenging, or impossible, to retrieve. Many worry about what happens to the fracking fluid and whether it contaminates drinking water, especially when fracking sites are close to homes and schools. As a result of these concerns, many countries have banned or halted fracking.

Protestors against fracking

Water contamination is an unintended consequence of using fossil fuels, and it impacts the health of countless species. For example, acid rain occurs when sulfur dioxides and nitrogen oxides are emitted into the atmosphere by the burning of fossil fuels through factory emissions and vehicle emissions. The sulfur dioxides and nitrogen oxides mix with water to form acids. When this acid rain falls or runs off surfaces, it can get into oceans, lakes, streams, and the ground, affecting the organisms that live there. Acid rain and other pollutants can also impact air quality and cause respiratory problems in species like humans. According to the World Health Organization (WHO), 93% of children under the age of 15 have their health endangered due to the air that they breathe. It's estimated that half a million children die each year from respiratory infections.

Some scientists believe nuclear energy is necessary if we are to reach very low carbon emissions, while others consider it to be an environmental disaster in the making. Nuclear power can be created because energy is stored in the bonds that hold the nucleus of an atom together. When bonds are split, large amounts of energy is released. This nuclear fission, or breaking apart within atoms, allows us to harvest nuclear energy. This process causes zero emissions and currently supplies 14% of the world's electricity. Some countries rely on nuclear energy heavily, such as France, which uses it for 75% of its electricity. While it is emission free, nuclear power isn't risk free. When natural disasters like earthquakes hit nuclear energy plants, the results can turn tragic. This happened in 2011 at the Fukushima Daiichi Nuclear Power Plant in Ōkuma after devastating earthquakes and tsunamis hit the country of Japan. The damaged power plant leaked water contaminated with radioactive isotopes, causing long-lasting negative consequences on human and ocean health. With natural disasters always possible, and with the damage that can occur when disasters combine with human technology like nuclear power, many people wonder if the risks outweigh the hoped-for benefits.

A nuclear power plant's cooling towers

Changes to Earth from earthquakes and volcanoes are called natural disasters because they're caused by Earth's tectonic plates, which have been shifting for billions of years. However, there's nothing natural about humans' impact on the climate and the crisis that we're causing. According to atmospheric scientist Eric Fetzer of NASA's Jet Propulsion Laboratory, "We've had 8,000 years of pretty much the same climate, and only about a century where things have really started to change." Because particles from the atmosphere are locked into thick ice that has built up over time, long cylinders cut from ice, called ice cores, give us valuable information about Earth's past. Ice cores from Antarctica allow us to look at long-term data, documenting 800,000 years of CO_2 levels in the atmosphere, while ice cores from Greenland provide data from up to 123,000 years ago. These show that CO_2 levels are currently 40% higher than they were before the industrial revolution began in the mid-eighteenth century. In 1800, atmospheric CO_2 was 283 parts per million. In 1960, the average atmospheric CO_2 was 317 parts per million, while in 2012 it was 394 parts per million. The rise can also be seen in the short term. In January of 2019, the monthly average of atmospheric carbon dioxide was 410.8 parts per million, whereas in January of 2020, the monthly average was 413.6 parts per million, and in January of 2021, it was 415.5 parts per million. If current trends continue, with an increase of about two parts per million a year, CO_2 concentrations will top 500 parts per million by 2050. This is roughly double the level that they were in preindustrial days. Because CO_2 traps heat and blocks it from escaping, it's estimated that the global temperature will rise, on average, between 3.5°F and 7°F by 2100.

While temperature change is part of Earth's history, the direct impact that humans have on adding greenhouse gases to the atmosphere is what makes current data so alarming. For example, the top six warmest years since humans have been recording temperature were 2015, 2016, 2017, 2018, 2019, and 2020. Overall, global surface temperature has increased by two degrees Fahrenheit since the 1880s. Two degrees sounds like a small overall temperature change, but it's significant because a global average of two degrees means the rise is actually much higher in some regions. Greater temperature increases in some areas mean more droughts and heat waves, with a serious impact on crops. The United Nations (UN) emphasizes the impact that such changes could have on sub-Saharan Africa, where temperatures are projected to increase faster than the global average. This conversation, however, goes far beyond location. *Environmental racism* refers to the systems in place that propel injustice through a disproportionate burden of intended or unintended environmental consequences and disadvantages for Black, Indigenous, and people of color. According to the UN, parts of Namibia and Botswana, both in Africa, are expected to experience the greatest temperature increases in the coming decades, which could lead to widespread food insecurity and starvation.

Rising temperatures will also cause Earth's ice to melt. According to the National Aeronautics and Space Administration (NASA), on average, 46 billion tons of ice from Alaskan glaciers melted each year from 2003 to 2010. This

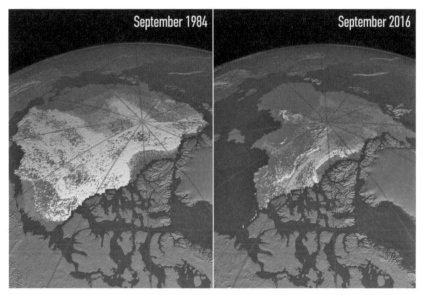

NASA's images of glacial melt from 1984 to 2016

is from Alaskan glaciers alone; there are also glaciers in a variety of countries including Canada, Russia, Pakistan, Iceland, Switzerland, Argentina, Austria, and Norway, as well as major glacial ice stores in Antarctica and Greenland. Through ice core data from the past 12,000 years, we know that Greenland has experienced cycles of thaw and freeze, but its ice cover is currently melting at some of its fastest rates. Between 1980 and 1990, Greenland lost 51 billion tons of ice, whereas between 2010 and 2018, there was a much higher loss, with 286 billion tons of ice melting or breaking off into the sea. As glaciers melt, ice that was once on land becomes water that can flow into the oceans, which leads to rising seas. In addition, like other substances, water expands as the seas grow warmer, which also contributes to rising sea levels.

Melting ice means habitat loss for species that live on the ice or depend on it for hunting. Polar bears spend months on the ice hunting seals. Today, they have become a symbol of what lost habitat can look like for species. Due to rising CO_2 levels and temperatures, polar bears' sea ice habitat is melting. Since 1996, the average Arctic temperature has increased by 7°F. Over the past 30 years, this warming has caused a 30% decline in sea ice cover in the Arctic. With less ice, it's more difficult for polar bears to hunt and breed, which impacts their survival. As a result, in 2008, polar bears were listed as a threatened species under the United States' Endangered Species Act.

Currently, 90% of the world's glaciers are shrinking, and sea levels are rising approximately 0.12 inches per year. By

Polar bears are a threatened species under the Endangered Species Act

2050, it's predicted that sea levels will rise 2.3 feet due to glacial melt. Many of the world's largest cities are located on the coast, including Mumbai, Shanghai, Buenos Aires, and New York City. There are also countless low-lying islands on Earth that will become fully or partially submerged, devastating their habitat for species that live there, including humans. However, the link between atmosphere and sea goes far beyond rising temperatures and sea levels; one of the biggest concerns is the impact that CO_2 has on ocean acidification.

The Republic of Maldives consists of 1,200 low-lying islands and is at great risk due to rising sea levels, including its capital Malé

Spotlight on Climate Change-makers

Marina Silva (born 1958) creates change through policy and activism. She grew up on a rubber plantation and learned to read and write as a teenager—the first to do so in her family. As a native Amazonian, she has been an active voice in policy about deforestation, especially illegal forestry in the Amazon rainforests. She has won the Goldman Environmental Prize for South & Central America and  has been named a "Champion of the Earth" by the United Nations. She ran for the president of Brazil in 2010, 2014, and 2018 with hopes of creating even greater change in Brazil by building an infrastructure around clean energy, such as wind and solar, to reduce greenhouse gas emissions.

Spotlight on Climate Change-makers

Nick Paul (born 1977) is a biologist and a professor of marine science. When cows eat grass, it ferments and makes methane, which cows release through burping and farting. On average, one cow releases one gallon of methane every 30 minutes. Methane is a greenhouse gas that is even more powerful than CO_2 at holding heat. Nick's research team found that adding a pink seaweed, Asparagopsis, to less than 1% of a cow's diet can significantly reduce their methane emissions. On a global scale, the addition of this seaweed to the diets of grazing farm animals could reduce global methane emissions by 10%.

Chapter 5

Land and Sea:

Deforestation and Ocean Acidification

The reality of our current climate crisis is unsettling. If nothing is done to change our policy and habits, our Earth will change so much that countless species will go extinct. All areas of Earth will be impacted; however, the first signs of unrecoverable change are already showing in the Arctic, the rainforest, and the ocean.

Left: the Arctic, right: the rainforest

There is more CO_2 in the air today than there has been in the past 800,000 years. And high CO_2 levels don't just cause rising temperatures. Unfortunately, it's much more complicated than that, because CO_2 doesn't just stay in the atmosphere—some of it is absorbed by the oceans. When CO_2 from the air dissolves in the water, it forms carbonic acid (H_2CO_3). Each year, Earth's oceans absorb approximately 25% of all CO_2 released by humans' burning of fossil fuels. As a result, oceans are acidifying faster than they have in the past 300 million years. Remember that during "the great dying", which occurred 252 million years ago, a massive increase of CO_2 occurred, which led to 90% of marine life and 70% of land life dying. Oceans are currently acidifying at a rate faster than they did during that extinction event—the world's biggest mass extinction.

The amount of hydrogen ion activity in a liquid is measured as pH (potential hydrogen). The pH scale goes from zero to 14, in which 7 is neutral. Anything below 7 is considered acidic, and anything above 7 is alkaline. Before the industrial revolution, Earth's surface water pH level was 8.2, and it's now at an average of 8.1. This may not seem like much, but according to the Environmental Protection Agency (EPA), it equates to the oceans being 25% more acidic (or less alkaline) than they were 200 years ago. As humans' population and greenhouse gas emissions increase, so increases the CO_2 in the atmosphere. Therefore, the oceans' pH continues to change.

Any fish tank owner knows that organisms in their tank have a range of tolerance in which they can survive. This range of tolerance can apply to salinity, temperature, dissolved oxygen, and pH levels. Now imagine a fish tank that's the size of the ocean—over 300,000 cubic miles. Just as fish tanks have a pH level at which organisms can no longer survive, so do the oceans. Research shows that for many species it's a pH level of 7.8. At our current rate of carbon absorption, oceans will reach this pH level in less than 100 years, by 2100. Just as young humans are vulnerable to air pollution, the young of aquatic species are particularly vulnerable to acidity. Some species will die as their body chemistry changes, and others because the acids cause them to dissolve.

Among the many marine species that will die at a pH level of 7.8 are those that form shells from calcium carbonate, $CaCO_3$. Biomineralization is the process of living organisms producing minerals. Many marine organisms, such as mollusks, produce minerals to form their shells. Calcium carbonate contains the mineral calcite, which reacts with acid. As water becomes more acidic, these calcifying organisms undergo a chemical reaction and their mineral parts begin to dissolve. You can show this reaction by dropping white vinegar, with a 2.5 pH level, onto the shells of calcifying organisms like oysters. When the vinegar and shell come in contact, an immediate chemical reaction of fizzing occurs. While a 2.5 pH is an extreme example, at a pH level of 7.8, many calcifying species will gradually die out. Some species currently showing this impact include coral.

Coral is made of hundreds of thousands of polyps, which are tiny marine organisms. The skeleton is made of calcium carbonate, which is vulnerable to acid. Australia's Great Barrier Reef is the world's largest coral reef system; it stretches over 1,400 miles and has an area of 133,000 square miles. It has 300-400 species of coral, but between the years of 1995 and 2017, half of its coral has been lost. The impact is particularly clear on the southern part of the reef due to temperature increases. Coral is an *indicator species*, one that gives information about the overall conditions of an environment. Indicator species are often the first impacted by the changing conditions of air or water quality in a habitat. The amount of coral currently dying serves as an environmental indicator for the changing surface temperatures and acidity levels of the ocean. Approximately 25% of all marine organisms rely on coral for shelter, food, mating territory and the nursery grounds that they create. And over half a billion people rely on coral-dependent fish for a significant portion of what they eat.

Healthy coral compared to coral with bleaching

It's estimated that around 2100, Earth's ocean surface levels will reach a pH level of 7.8. Depending on your age, you may be alive then; so within your lifetime (and/or your children's) the ocean may well hit what we call its tipping point. A tipping point is the critical point of change, which can be difficult or impossible to recover. This impact will lead to more and more *dead zones*—areas of water that can't support life—which will lead to crippling effects on the food chain and the ocean's biodiversity.

Carbon naturally cycles and stores in nature, with the carbon cycle continuously transferring carbon due to photosynthesis, decomposition, respiration, and combustion. Carbon is found in fossil fuels and is found in Earth's atmosphere and ocean. Carbon also stores in animals, and in plants due to photosynthesis. Plants that range from microscopic algae in the oceans to the giant Sequoia trees on the western slopes of the Sierra Nevada capture CO_2 from the atmosphere and store it. Currently, the estimate is that trees and land plants absorb 25% of all CO_2 released by humans' burning of fossil fuels (the same amount as

the ocean). Together, the ocean and plants absorb 50% of the CO_2 we release, but that leaves a significant amount of excess CO_2 in the atmosphere, which is why atmospheric CO_2 levels are rising each year.

The act of planting trees and letting them grow until they are mature will help reduce Earth's greenhouse gas concentrations and ocean acidification. According to the global tree restoration report, if trees were planted globally in an area that adds up to the size of the United States, it would reduce CO_2 in the atmosphere by up to 25%. Yet, when trees are burned as a strategy of slash-and-burn deforestation or by naturally occurring or human started fires, the CO_2 that was captured by the trees and stored is released back into the atmosphere. Deforestation through cutting and burning releases more than 1.5 billion tons of CO_2 back into the atmosphere each year, an estimated 15% of greenhouse gas emissions.

Trees being planted in Seychelles

On average, 15 billion trees are cut down each year. Since humans have been on Earth, the amount of trees has reduced by approximately 46%. Tropical rainforests, which make up 6% of Earth's land surface, are one of the regions in which the impact of deforestation can be seen most. In the past 50 years, about 17% of the Amazon rainforests have been deforested through cutting or burning. Not only does this affect the air, and as a result, the oceans, but deforestation also impacts the species that live in or rely on the trees. There are 16,000 different tree species in the Amazon rainforest, which has so much biodiversity that in one three-acre plot, there could be 650 different types of trees. Imagine all of the shelter and food these trees provide for countless other organisms. Yet, they're being destroyed at an unprecedented rate. Forests around the world are split into various sized sections, called forest fragments. Forest fragmentation has happened from the development of everything from roads to farms to cities to soccer fields.

More developed land, which has trees harvested or construction on the land, means less CO_2 being captured by trees. More CO_2 leads to more ocean acidification. And these habitat changes are causing more and more species to become endangered or extinct.

Deforestation in New Zealand

Spotlight on Climate Change-makers

Wangari Maathai (1940-2011) won the 2004 Nobel Peace Prize and founded The Green Belt Movement organization. This grass-roots movement, started in Kenya, focuses on training women to learn communi-ty-based forestry. As a result of Maathai's work, millions of trees have been planted, bringing ecological benefits and also social and economic benefits by empow-ering and employing women. One of Maathai's most famous quotes is, "When we plant trees, we plant the seeds of peace and hope."

Spotlight on Climate Change-makers

Emma Camp (born 1987) is a coral biologist and a marine bio-geochemist who works both at a university and at the Great Barrier Reef. She focuses on finding and growing corals that are more resilient to climate change. Her research is done through the Coral Nurture Program where scientists use coral gardening to  encourage healthy coral to grow so it can then be transplanted elsewhere.

Chapter 6

Human-Caused Extinctions

Extinctions are a part of Earth's history. There have been extinctions for far longer than *Homo sapiens* has existed. However, countless extinctions have also been caused by *Homo sapiens*. Early *Homo sapiens* left a long history of traveling to new locations and causing native species to go extinct. In chapter eight, you will learn about invasive species. In many ways, *Homo sapiens* are a highly effective invasive species, because when we relocate, we take over other species' native environment and cause great harm.

A model of a Neanderthal from the Neanderthal Museum in Germany

One of the earliest examples of *Homo sapiens* causing an extinction of a species was to our species' closest known relative, the Neanderthal. Neanderthals, *Homo neanderthalensis*, walked upright, used tools, and had a brain similar in size to ours. Evidence shows that when *Homo sapiens* arrived in what is now Europe, 40,000 years ago, the Neanderthals went extinct. It's unclear if *Homo sapiens* outcompeted the Neanderthals for resources or outright killed them, but what is clear is that the two species mated. We know this because DNA testing done today shows that many people now alive are up to 4% Neanderthal. That means that *you* could be part Neanderthal and that your *Homo sapiens* ancestors may have caused your Neanderthal ancestors to go extinct. But, it's not just you; *Homo sapiens* have caused lots of species' relatives to go extinct.

Homo sapiens' pattern of migration, relocation, and then causing the extinction of species continued around the globe. Their effect can be seen with Earth's megafauna, which is the term used for large land animals. As *Homo sapiens* arrived from one continent to the next, soon afterward the megafauna went extinct.

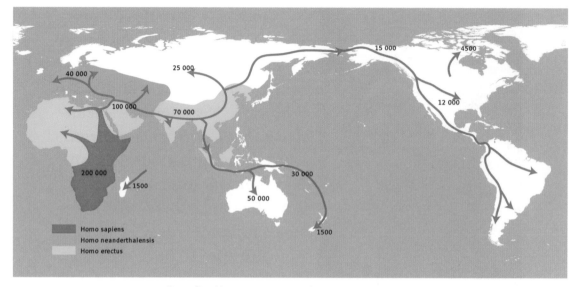

Spreading Homo sapiens over the past 200,000 years

One example is the diprotodon, the largest known marsupial, which lived in Australia and looked like a 10-foot long, seven-foot high wombat. The species is estimated to have existed from 1.6 million years ago to 44,000 years ago, while many scientists believe that *Homo sapiens* settled on the continent of Australia approximately 50,000 years ago. The diprotodon was doing fine for over one and a half million years until *Homo sapiens* came along. Chris Johnson wrote a book entitled *Australia's Mammal Extinctions: a 50,000 year history*, and noted that *Homo sapiens'*

A model of a diprotodon in the Natural History Museum in London

early extinctions were most likely unintentional. Johnson stated that if one group of ten hunters killed one diprotodon a year, within approximately 700 years, every diprotodon within a few hundred miles would be dead. This is where perspective is key. Johnson explained that *Homo sapiens* probably didn't notice the decline of the species because it happened slowly over generations. Unaware of how many diprotodons once lived, humans would continue expanding their territory and this pattern would continue until one by one the diprotodons were all gone.

The same thing happened in New Zealand, a country of islands over 2,000 miles from Australia. Before humans inhabited New Zealand, the moa, a 12-foot-tall, flightless bird that could weigh 500 pounds, only had one predator, the Haast's eagle. The Haast's eagle was a raptor with a 9-foot wingspan and talons almost 2.5 inches long and a hallux (or big toe) claw that was over 4 inches long.

A reconstruction of a moa in 1903, approximately 450 years after they went extinct

Within a few hundred years of humans' arrival, or some even estimate within 100 years, humans hunted the moas to extinction. With the moas' extinction, so came the extinction of the Hasst's eagle.

The same pattern occurred around the world. The megatherium, a South American giant ground sloth that was

20 feet long from head to tail, went extinct around 12,000 years ago. This extinction coincides with when *Homo sapiens* migrated to that part of South America. Critics argue that the correlation of human arrival time when megafauna went extinct does not directly show that *Homo sapiens* caused the extinction. Scientists' conclusions, however, are based both on evidence they collect and on inferences they make based on what's currently happening to our best example of modern-day megafauna, the elephant. Elephants in both Asia and Africa are currently vulnerable to extinction due to habitat loss and poaching.

A drawing of the skeletal remains of a megatherium

The Asian elephant was listed as an endangered species in 1976 and the African elephant was listed in 1978. For Asian elephants, reproduction doesn't begin until around the age of 14, and females have a long gestation period. Mammoths, which went extinct after *Homo sapiens* settled in North America, seem to have had a similar gestation period

An African bush elephant

to elephants, 18-22 months. Moreover, elephants typically have only one baby at a time, meaning that even at the best of times, elephant populations grow slowly. During the time before maturity, elephants are particularly vulnerable to predators. Elephants are currently in danger of extinction despite humans currently having protections in place for them. Imagine a time before technology, data collection, government policy, conservation land, and non-profit organizations dedicated to saving a species, and it's easy to see why megafauna of the past were so vulnerable to extinction.

With extinctions of the past, it was hard to understand what was happening until it was too late. Yet, today people understand that we are currently causing species to die. Since 1964, IUCN, which stands for International Union for Conservation of Nature, has kept a red list of the status of species, listing them as extinct, extinct in the wild, critically endangered, endangered, vulnerable, near threatened, conservation-dependent, and least concern. Out of all assessed species, IUCN believes 27% are currently threatened with extinction.

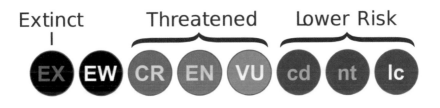

The IUCN's Red List of Threatened Species indicator system

Historically, on Earth one species of mammals has gone extinct every 700 years. In just the last century, the following mammals have been declared extinct: the Tasmanian wolf, also known as the Tasmanian tiger, which was a carnivorous marsupial; the Baiji dolphin, a freshwater dolphin found in China's Yangtze River; the Pinta tortoise, a species of Galápagos tortoise; the Golden toad, found in Costa Rica's Monteverde Cloud Forest Reserve; the Caribbean monk seal, which could grow up to eight feet long; the Caspian tiger, a tiger which could weigh up to 530 pounds; the Formosan clouded leopard, a species that lost its habitat due to logging; the Pyrenean ibex, which looked like a wild goat, and whose males had thick curved horns; and the Toolache wallaby, a nocturnal species which was known for being social and for seeking food in the twilight hours. In 2013, a new species of mammal was discovered, the olinguito, which lives in the Andes Mountains and is part of the raccoon family. It's currently on the IUCN's list of threatened species.

Homo sapiens' closest living relative today is the chimpanzee. While there are over seven billion humans on Earth, there are only 150,000 to 250,000 chimpanzees left in the wild. Chimpanzees are currently listed as an endangered species. Some of Earth's other species currently in danger of going extinct include half of all amphibians, one-quarter of all mammals, one-fifth of all reptiles, and one-sixth of all birds.

Part of why extinction is happening so rapidly is that in a single century *Homo sapiens'* population has doubled, then doubled again, and then again. In 1920, there were around

1,800,000,000 humans, whereas in 2021, there were around 7,800,000,000 and by 2100, it's projected that there will be 11,000,000,000. With more people come more habitat loss, more CO_2 emissions, and more ocean acidification. All of this change is happening quickly. And, just as Darwin found, when species have characteristics that are less adapted to a changing environment, they are less likely to survive and reproduce. That is why more species are going extinct.

Spotlight on Climate Change-makers

Giulia C.S. Good Stefani (born 1979) is a lawyer who uses her background to defend marine mammals in need. She led a lawsuit to save the vaquita, the world's smallest and most endangered porpoise. These porpoises drown when they are caught in gillnets used by the fishing industry to catch other fish, and the court case won a ban on those fish. Giulia also fights to protect the Southern Resident orcas. These orcas are in danger of extinction because there are not enough salmon to eat. She is working to restore salmon back to abundance in the Columbia River for the hungry orcas.

Spotlight on Climate Change-makers

At ten years old, **Sofia Molina** (born 2009) founded a non-profit organization in Mexico called *Cococu*, which is named after the first syllables of her favorite words: conscientizar (to make aware), conocer (to know) and cuidar (to care). She advocates at international forums for children's perspectives to be taken into account when making decisions about the environment. Sofia also educates children about activism with a focus on protecting habitats. To date, her organization's efforts have conserved over 30,000 acres of land.

Chapter 7

Unintended Consequences and Plastic

U nintended consequences are results or impacts that are unexpected and usually negative or harmful. In the 1950s, before Rachel Carson's *Silent Spring* was published, a series of unintended consequences from use of the pesticide DDT occurred on the island country of Borneo. The story began when the native people, the Dayak, experienced an outbreak of malaria, which is spread by mosquitoes. Borneo's malaria outbreak was so bad that the World Health Organization (WHO) recommended that the government spray widely with DDT. The DDT killed the mosquitoes, which stopped the spread of malaria. However, an unintended consequence was that other insects also ingested the DDT. The island's geckos eat insects, and as a result, the geckos also ate the DDT. Cats on the island then ate the geckos and ended up dying from the toxins. With fewer cats, the rat population on the island increased. The increase in rats led to the spread of sylvatic plague and typhus, two diseases deadly to humans, on the island. As a result, the World Health Organization decided to airdrop in cats, in what is often called *Operation Cat Drop*, to the island to help control the rat population. This shows how a series of unintended consequences can occur from one initial decision.

A gecko from Borneo

Another example of unintended consequences happened in Mono Lake, California—a saltwater lake near Nevada's border. The lake is about two and a half times saltier than the ocean. It is home to brine shrimp, which flourish in water with a salinity level of 35 to 40 parts per thousand. Annually, over two million migratory birds visit Mono lake and eat the brine shrimp and alkali flies, which are flies adapted to the salty, alkaline water. Islands in Mono Lake also serve as important breeding and nesting grounds for birds because they're safe from predators. Some birds that rely on this habitat are California gulls, eared grebes, and phalaropes. This unique ecosystem was thriving until humans made a decision in the early 1900s.

Mono Lake

The growing city of Los Angeles needed more water, so an aqueduct system, hundreds of miles long, was built between the Owens River in Eastern Sierra Nevada Mountains and Los Angeles. An aqueduct is a structure that allows flowing water to travel from one location to another. In the 1940s, the water was diverted from tributary streams that fed into Mono Lake. As a result, Mono Lake's water levels went down, which doubled the salinity levels, impacting the brine shrimp, the alkali flies, and the entire food web. The lake dropped over 40 vertical feet, making land bridges to the islands, allowing predators like foxes to kill birds and their eggs. These unintended consequences of human action led to a changed habitat and the loss of species. After an ecological study in 1976 documented the devastation from the diverted water, the community rallied in support of the lake. It took eighteen years, but after activists brought various lawsuits, in 1994, the State Water Resources Control Board decided unanimously to divert less water. Over time, this decision has allowed Mono Lake's water levels to rise slowly and species to return.

There are countless other environmental examples of unforeseen consequences. One of the most significant examples over the past century has been the use of plastic. There are a range of types of plastic, from polyethylene (PET), which is a polyester, to polystyrene (PS), which is often made into a foam, to polyvinyl chloride (PVC), which is made into pipes and flooring. Plastic is not natural. Plastics are made from things that are natural, such as cellulose, coal, and natural gas; however, they have to undergo a manufactured process of polymerization, the joining together of monomers, or single molecules, to form polymers. As a result of polymerization, plastic doesn't easily break down. According to the Environmental Protection Agency (EPA), it takes 100-400 years for plastic to decompose in a landfill; however, some scientists estimate breakdown takes far longer. Because plastic was invented in the early 1900s and began to be used widely in the 1960s, not enough time has passed to fully understand its long-term impact.

Recycling plastic into new plastic uses two-thirds the amount of energy that it would have taken to make the plastic from raw materials. Other items have a much higher recovery rate when recycled, such as aluminum. Making new aluminum out of recycled aluminum uses 5% of the energy that it would take to make it from all new materials. Currently, 50% of all plastic is made for single-use products and packaging that can't be recycled.

Plastic being sorted for recycling

It's plastic's inability to break down that has made it so popular. Plastic began to be used in place of glass because it's both durable and lightweight. Plastic then expanded to everyday uses from plastic forks to six-pack rings. Because it's affordable, it started to be used widely in all areas of industry from hospitals to fishing gear to product packaging. It's currently used everywhere, even in places you can't see, from piping below ground to improving space exploration. Plastic can be used to help the environment by improving the R-Value—a material's resistance to heat flow—of products like insulation, and it's lighter for the shipment of goods, which can reduce fossil fuel use. It can even be made to repel or kill bacteria, making it important for medical use. Right now there are even plastic vials containing the DNA of species that are on the verge of going extinct.

While there are numerous benefits of plastic, there are also unintended consequences. One of the major consequences is the potential health impact of BPA, bisphenol-A, one of the chemicals used to make and harden plastics starting in the 1960s. BPA from bottles and packaging can leak into food and beverages. Some experts believe that BPA acts like the hormone estrogen in the body. Two studies have found adults with higher BPA have a higher rate of heart problems, and BPA is particularly dangerous for infants and young children because of effects on the brain. As a result, in 2012, the U.S Food and Drug Administration (FDA) banned BPA in baby bottles and sippy cups.

PFAS, Per- and Polyfluoroalkyl Substances, which contain toxic chemicals, are also used in the manufacturing of plastic. They have been nicknamed "forever chemicals" because they could take hundreds, possibly even thousands, of years to break down. PFAS are commonly found in fast food packaging because they are grease and water-resistant. This is particularly dangerous because the packaging is holding food, which people then eat, ingesting chemicals along the way. Because the chemicals don't break down, they stay in the body. PFAS have been linked to kidney and testicular cancer, thyroid disease, hormone disruption, decreased fertility, lower birth weights, higher cholesterol, and impact on the nervous system. In 2019, the "Keep Food Containers Safe from PFAS Act" passed the House of Representatives, but it's yet to be passed by the Senate. As a result, many states are passing their own bills to protect people from PFAS.

However, the impact of plastic goes far beyond humans' health. According to the National Oceanic and Atmospheric Administration (NOAA), plastics are the most common marine debris found in Earth's oceans and Great Lakes. According to PlasticsEurope, in 2018, almost 400 million tons of plastic were produced worldwide. It's estimated that between 5.3 million and 14 million tons were littered, intentionally or unintentionally, into the oceans.

Plastic litter on a beach

According to the United Nations, there are on average 46,000 pieces of plastic in one square mile of ocean. Some plastic breaks down in the ocean, releasing BPA and other chemicals; it can also break into smaller pieces known as microplastics, which are less than five millimeters in size. Microplastics are often so small that they pass through filters, which means that there is potential for them to end up in humans' water supply for drinking and agricultural use. As of 2018, microplastics had been found in 114 different water species. Because plastics are not digestible, these microplastics are dangerous for the creatures that eat them, and the animals that eat the species with microplastics in their organs.

Microplastics are not the only issue; large pieces of plastic in water are also problematic. Of the millions of tons of plastic in the ocean, much of it does not break down. Ocean gyres, which are circular ocean currents formed from the wind, carry items like plastic to a common location or locations. The largest patch, the Great Pacific Garbage Patch—also known as the Pacific trash vortex—is currently in the northern part of the Pacific Ocean and is estimated to hold over 1.8 trillion pieces of plastic. As of 2018, researchers estimated it to be twice the size of Texas. It's estimated that 54% of the litter comes from North America and Asia and 20% from boats, ships, and oil rigs. With so much visible pollution floating on the surface, an alarming estimate is that 70% of marine plastic debris sinks deep below the surface and is no longer visible.

Microplastics

According to the EPA, the category of trash containing the most plastic is containers and packaging, with 14 million tons thrown away in 2017. This category includes single-use plastic bags, which are easily blown by the wind and commonly found in waterways. Single-use plastic bags were introduced in the late 1970s as an alternative to paper bags because they were more durable. However, a paper bag decomposes in about a month, whereas a plastic bag takes much, much longer. The durability of plastic is why it's popular, but also why it can harm the environment for such a long time.

Each year, over a trillion plastic bags are used worldwide. These bags have been known to clog drainage systems, which can lead to flooding. Animals also eat plastic bags on land and in the water. One of the best-documented examples of the unintended consequences of single-use plastic bags is on sea turtles. When plastic bags float suspended in the ocean, they look like jellyfish or algae. According to the World Wildlife Fund (WWF), a green sea turtle that en-counters a plastic bag will eat it 62% of the time. When ingested, plastic bags can block sea turtles' intestinal organs, causing them to die from ruptured organs or starvation. Green sea turtles are currently listed as an endangered species.

An art exhibit that shows how plastic bags look like jellyfish

Since 2018, more plastic is currently ending up in landfills and as litter due to a policy change in China. Starting in the 1990s, China took recycling, especially plastic, from around the world. They sent ships filled with products to countries around the world, and rather than returning with empty ships, they paid for the country's recycling and brought it back to China. There, cheap labor forces cleaned the recycling and made it into new products that China could sell. Once such product was fleece, which is made out of a type of plastic, a polyester called polyethylene terephthalate (PET). China bought approximately 12.6 billion pounds of plastic a year. Then, on January 1 2018, China started the "National Sword" policy banning recycled plastic from other countries. Part of the reason for the ban is that the recycling was contaminated. People weren't cleaning their bottles and jars, and they mixed in items that shouldn't be recycled. As a result, today, even when people think they're recycling, some towns and cities put recycling in the landfill because it costs them more to clean, sort, and recycle plastic than to throw it away.

Plastic production leads to a lot of waste and greenhouse gases. The EPA estimates that one ounce of CO_2 is produced for every ounce of polyethylene (PET) produced, creating a 1:1 ratio of use. Other sources estimate a much higher amount of CO_2 for every ounce of PET, as high as a 5:1 ratio. PET is one of the most common forms of plastic, used in the packaging of food and drinks and everything from shampoo to tennis balls.

Manufacturing plastic leads to unintended consequences of harming species' health and releasing CO_2. And CO_2 rise leads to the unintended consequences of altering the composition of Earth's atmosphere and acidifying the oceans, which has further unintended consequences on the health of Earth's species.

Spotlight on Climate Change-makers

Anna Du (born 2005) entered a STEM competition at twelve years old and built a remote-operated vehicle (ROV) that can find microplastics on the ocean floor. Her design detects plastic, making it easier to collect later on. Anna's currently working on getting a patent for her design.

Spotlight on Climate Change-makers

Laura Marston (born 1979) is the owner of Gogo Refill, a store that helps cut down on plastic use. Customers bring their own refillable containers, such as mason jars or empty shampoo bottles, and refill them with eco-friendly cleaning and beauty products. Customers pay by the product's weight and in just one year, the store prevented the purchase of 20,000 products packaged in plastic.

Chapter 8

Invasive Species and the *New Pangaea*

One of the most significant examples of unintended consequences is the spread of invasive species. Invasive species are organisms that are relocated to somewhere new that is not their natural habitat, and that cause environmental and economic harm in the new location. Invasive species are among the greatest threats to other species; they can take over their habitat, make them sick, eat food they would have eaten, or eat them. According to the U.S. Fish & Wildlife Service, there are approximately 50,000 non-native species currently in the United States, of which 4,300 are considered invasive species. Currently, there are non-native and invasive species on every continent.

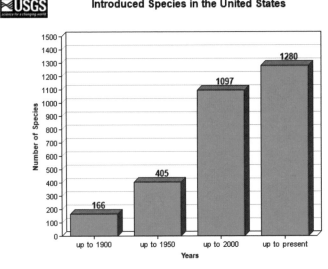

(graph created: 6/5/2021 8:19:42 PM by the United States Geological Survey)

A graph showing species introduced to the United States since 1900

Unlike Earth's supercontinent of the past, Pangea, where the land of all continents was combined, today, Earth's continents and islands create geographic isolation for countless land species. Or so they should. With some continents over 5,000 miles apart, evolutionarily, species should only be able to travel as far as their wings, fins, feet, or seeds could take them. Early humans, for example, took thousands, even tens of thousands of years, to travel far distances across continents. Yet, this is no longer the case, as humans currently travel across continents in hours or around the whole planet in days. Moreover, when humans make these trips by plane and ship, they are often not alone—intentionally or unintentionally, they bring other species along with them. Biologists call this globalization, or international fluidity across continents, the *New Pangaea.*

The problem with the New Pangaea is that species that relocate may leave their predators and natural competitors behind. They can also carry diseases and parasites with them. Some relocated species aren't adapted for their new environment and quickly die, but others, free of predators and resistant to the disease they have imported, can multiply wildly and crowd out native species. As a result, invasive species, species that invade a new ecosystem, can impact ecosystems' biodiversity and disrupt the economy. There are countless examples of the impact and unintended consequences of invasive species around the world, but we'll focus on seven examples, one from each continent.

In Australia, a wealthy landowner arranged for 13 European rabbits to be shipped over to his homestead in 1859. Rabbits are not native to Australia, yet as a result of these purposely introduced rabbits, there are now an estimated 200 million rabbits in Australia. On average, the rabbits brought

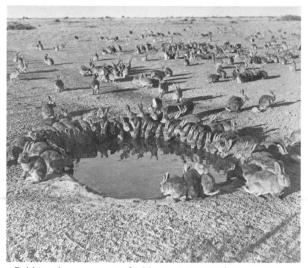

Rabbits, that were part of a Myxoma virus trial, at a watering hole in Australia in 1938

into Australia had four litters a year with five rabbits per litter (there's an expression "breeding like rabbits" for a reason). The high rate of reproduction, and relative absence of predators, meant that the population size compounded again and again. The rabbits destroyed crops and caused devastating economic impacts. Their overgrazing of the land led to less food for native species and caused soil to erode. In response, the government has tried everything from releasing rabbits infected with a virus to spread and kill other rabbits, to poison, to controlled fires to help decrease the population.

Antarctica is the most isolated of the continents, yet it's still susceptible to invasive species. In just one tourist season, on the bottom of their shoes tourists unintentionally brought about 70,000 seeds with them. Antarctica has only two native vascular plants; now, due to travelers, the *Poa annua* is a third plant that has established itself. Seeds are not the only transported organisms. An insect, *Eretmoptera murphyi*, a flightless midge, is now on Antarctica's Signy Island. These insects are digging into the soil and starting to change the ecosystem of the island. As travel to Antarctica becomes easier and more desirable due to warming temperatures, more tourists will come. A fear has mounted that marine invertebrates, such as mussels, will hitchhike on the hulls of ships and become another invasive species, since they spread quickly and live in cold water. The tourists, who journey from all over the world, will unintentionally bring with them more and more invasive species.

Africa's Nile Perch is an example of a species that was

purposefully introduced for economic gain. These fish can grow up to six feet long and weigh 240 pounds. As a result, they are exciting to catch and they serve as an important food source. The Nile perch are native to Ethiopia, but in 1962, people brought them into Lake Victoria, the continent's largest lake. The

Nile Perch

Nile perch reproduced easily and quickly became the lake's dominant predatory fish. As a result of the number of Nile perch and the impact of the parasites they carry on their body, over 300 native fish of Lake Victoria are no longer found in the lake.

One of the 4,300 invasive species in North America is the green crab. The species is from Europe and most likely traveled in the hull of a ship to Massachusetts, where it was first observed in 1817. Once green crabs arrive in a location, they can spread through migration on surface currents. Currently, they are found on North America's east coast from South Carolina to Newfoundland.

Green crab in Maine

On the west coast, they quickly expanded over 450 miles in 10 years; they are now found from San Francisco to British Columbia. It's projected that they will soon spread up to parts of Alaska and down to Mexico. Green crabs have a large diet, including young clams, oysters, and mussels, which has both economic and environmental impacts. On just the East Coast, it's estimated that green crabs cost the fishing industry 19 million dollars a year.

In Japan, the common snapping turtle was originally introduced as a pet in the 1960s. These turtles live on average to be 15-20 years old and lay approximately 20-30 eggs at a time. Adult snapping turtles weigh on average 23 pounds and eat so much they have altered their new habitats. At a mature size they have few to no predators. In Japan, the snapping turtles eat native fish, birds, reptiles, and small mammals, disrupting the entire food web. They

The common snapping turtle

eat fish and fishing nets, which harms the local economy. They also bite and injure people. Purchasing animals from faraway places to keep as pets often leads to the introduction of invasive species when the animals escape or are released by their owners.

Despite amphibians being one of the more endangered categories of animals, the African clawed frog, native to sub-Saharan Africa, is now spreading throughout the world.

These frogs were brought to Chile for laboratory use, and in the early 1980s, they were released into the wild. They can live up to fifteen years and can outcompete native frogs with their huge appetites for frogs, fish, and birds. Even worse, they can be a vector that carries parasites and other diseases. A vector can transmit a disease from one species to the next. For example, African clawed frogs are tolerant to the fungus chytridiomycosis but can carry and transmit it to other frogs, where the skin disease becomes deadly. One study out of the University of Maryland shows that in cool, moist conditions, chytridiomycosis can kill up to 80% of vulnerable frogs in a single year.

In Europe, the Asian hornet was accidentally brought to France in 2003 from China in cargo. The hornet is spreading its territory at a rate of 35 to 50 miles a year. Country borders make no difference to invasive species; as a result, the Asian hornet has already expanded throughout much of Europe. The Asian hornet preys upon honeybees and other pollinating insects. As a result, the hornets are driving down populations of these species, some of which were already endangered. With fewer pollinators, the economy is impacted. Pollinators are essential to agriculture because they move pollen from the male portion of flowers, the

An Asian hornet

anthers, to the female portion, the stigma. This pollination is necessary for the growth of many fruit and nut trees as well as other crops. The Asian hornet can also be aggressive toward people. As a result, the French government spent over 10 million Euros in one year (approximately 12 million dollars) destroying their nests.

All of these examples of invasive species reached their new home because of *Homo sapiens*. We go everywhere and we take other species with us. Therefore, humans should also be considered an invasive species. Our impact is constant. Looking back from the extinctions of megafauna to today's species, humans take over and alter habitats around the world. Yet, we *Homo sapiens* are also vulnerable. The *New Pangaea* has also allowed viruses to spread rapidly around the world. This rapid spread allows pandemics to occur; a pandemic is a disease or infection that spreads geographically over multiple continents or the entire world. Viruses evolve and change, making them an ongoing health and economic concern. In 2020, the dangers of the *New Pangaea* were felt worldwide when the coronavirus virus SARS-CoV-2, which causes COVID-19, caused a pandemic within months of the virus being discovered. You can see that the daily transport of people, animals, plants, and goods from continent to continent creates deadly, unintended consequences for all species, including *Homo sapiens*.

Spotlight on Climate Change-makers

Peter Alsip (born 1993) is a scientist who works for the University of Michigan's Cooperative Institute for Great Lakes Research. His research brings attention to how climate change makes Lake Michigan more vulnerable to invasive Asian carp. Peter's research suggests that as climate change warms the waters of the Great Lakes, it will increase summer food availability at the surface and allow these fishes to feed more actively. Climate change increases the chance of Asian carp surviving, establishing itself, and disrupting the ecology and economy of the Great Lakes.

Spotlight on Climate Change-makers

Andrew McCullough (born 1983) is a high school biology and marine science teacher who takes his classroom beyond the school walls to teach his students about the invasive green crab's negative impacts on Maine's coast. McCullough's classes engage in field research in the tidal zones of the bay, which is one mile from their school. His students have trapped thousands of green crabs and collected data since 2014. Each spring, students also plant 15,000 native clam seeds to help the bay's environmental and economic recovery.

Chapter 9

Profit Over Planet: The Cost of Greed

The next factor putting Earth in danger is greed. The data showing humans' impact on Earth over the range of topics discussed in this book is widely available, yet too many people deny that it's happening. Those who deny it often have an agenda, which is typically money or power. Some companies, like those in the fossil fuel industry, deny humans' role in our climate crisis because they're biased. Their income and stock value is based on the success of fossil fuels, so they're unwilling to acknowledge their company's role in climate change and do everything that they can to dismiss the evidence. *Profit over people* is a term used by Noam Chomsky, a scholar and writer, to explain the systems in place, both economically and politically, that support the profit of companies while ignoring the needs of people.

The fossil fuel industry has *a lot* of money. In 2019, Exxon Mobile's total assets were worth over 360 billion dollars, and the company employed 74,900 people. Exxon Mobil is consistently listed as one of the *Fortune* 500, Fortune magazine's annual list of the largest and most profitable companies. Companies and industries with a lot of money often have the means, through lobbying and donations, to influence politi-

The U.S. Capitol Building

cians. Politicians are the ones who can pass laws that put restrictions on greenhouse gas emissions, or that protect endangered species, or that give tax credits to those who use alternative energy sources. Or, politicians can pass laws that make it easier for environmental damage to continue. In an ideal world, politicians would vote based on what's best for people and the planet. They would be educated about topics and lead us in the right direction. Unfortunately, systems are in place that allow greed, power, and money to corrupt politics.

Much of the money that goes to politicians comes from campaign donors. For many politicians, their biggest donors are lobbyists. Lobbyists' job is to advocate for a cause in an effort to influence how politicians vote. In theory, they do so by providing important information to lawmakers. However, information is often skewed in support of their employer. As a result, voting is not always based on evidence or ethics; too often, it's influenced by money. In the 2018 midterm election, the fossil fuel industry spent over $359 million dollars on campaign donations and lobbying. Individual members of Congress who have received the most–millions of dollars–in donations from the fossil fuel industry are consistently the politicians who deny or dismiss the evidence around our climate crisis and vote for legislation that supports the fossil fuel industry.

Campaign signs for people running for political office

Why is campaign money so important to politicians? They use it to run their campaign (think about all those political ads you see on TV) against opponents who typically have far less campaign money. Because incumbent politicians are often financially backed by lobbyists, they usually have more money. As a result, they win office again; then, as long as they vote "correctly," they get more money from lobbyists, and the cycle continues. This happens with both Republicans and Democrats and concerning all issues on the political spectrum, including renewable energy. The difference is one of scale. In 2017-2018, lobbyists for renewable energy spent $1 for every $13 spent by the fossil fuel industry's efforts through lobbying and campaign donations.

Part of why lobbyists focus so much time and money on members of Congress is that, unlike the president, who can only serve two terms, members of the U.S. House of Representatives and U.S. Senate don't have term limits. They can serve as many terms as they're re-elected to. Therefore, the cycle of lobbyists' money fueling campaigns has led to long-lasting politicians and long-lasting policies.

Another example of lobbyists' impact is which industries or causes receive subsidies. Subsidies include tax breaks and direct payments for research and development to help companies or organizations thrive. In 2017, 5.2 trillion dollars ($5,200,000,000,000) was spent worldwide on fossil fuel subsidies. Much of this money goes toward reducing the prices that customers pay for fossil fuels by lowering fossil fuel companies' taxes and, therefore, distorting the market. Without these subsidies, the high cost of fossil fuels might propel people to move toward alternative energy sources, like solar and wind energy. Sometimes, governments that want to promote the use of these alternate energy sources will use subsidies to promote them too, such as by providing a rebate to people who install solar batteries or buy electric vehicles. These subsidies give people incentives and money to invest in new industries. But these subsidies are vulnerable, and lobbyists for fossil fuel companies often oppose them.

Protestors against fossil fuel subsidies

An analogy to help show how government subsidies prevent people from moving away from fossil fuels is by comparing it to watching a movie at home. Until the 1970s, if you wanted to watch a movie at home, you could only see movies shown on television—with most homes having between four and seven options of channels. Then in 1976, VHS, Video Home System, allowed you to watch movies on video or what were called VHS tapes. For two decades, people were delighted with VHS and the ability to rent or buy movies so as to be able to watch movies of their own choosing. Then in 1996, DVDs, Digital Video Discs, which were smaller and showed higher quality images, became available to the public. Some people resisted this change, with many focusing on the fact that they had invested in VHS players and tapes. Still, over time, DVD players became the primary tool to use to watch movies. Stores where you could rent movies slowly shifted from VHS to DVD. But what if the government gave subsidies to the VHS industry, making their products cheaper than they actually should have been? Would the shift to DVD have ever happened? Where would our technology be today if we'd been encouraged financially to stay with VHS players? The shift has currently happened to watching movies digitally, which requires neither VHS or DVD players. Change happens if artificial forces don't hold it back.

There are countries and politicians embracing this change and becoming leaders in environmental policy. Sweden has set a goal of having 100% of their energy come from renewable sources by 2040. They are actively working toward this goal, and as of 2018, 54% of their energy came from renewable sources. By comparison, in the United States only 11% of energy comes from renewable sources.

Much in the way the pesticide industry hired scientists to claim that Rachel Carson's book *Silent Spring* was a hoax, the same thing is happening today. In 2015, journalists reported that a scientist, Dr. Willie Soon, was paid over 1.2 million dollars in funding by some leaders of the fossil fuel industry. They funded him in exchange for making inaccurate claims that it's primarily the Sun's energy that has caused Earth's climate to change and that little impact has come from humans. The fossil fuel industry spent over 48 million dollars from 1997 to 2010 on similar efforts to deny that fossil fuels play a role in Earth's climate crisis.

As a result of some powerful groups spreading lies and disinformation about climate change, the topic has become political and polarizing. Earth's climate crisis is not a "hoax." The climate crisis is a complex problem that impacts all parts of our lives ranging from the economy to transportation to food production to public health. If we don't change our policies and priorities, the climate crisis will grow into a widespread humanitarian crisis, as more extreme weather, wildfires, and floods destroy homes, habitats, and crops. The humans impacted the most will be determined based on geography and poverty. From there, the challenges will broaden as changes to the atmosphere, ocean acidity levels, deforestation, and our planet's species diversity continues. The climate crisis won't be easy to overcome, but the first step is admitting that there is a problem.

And that problem is *us*.

Eventually, there will be so much evidence, and potentially so much environmental injustice and tragedy, that the truth can no longer be denied. This is when profit over people becomes *profit over planet*. If we stay on the track of letting profit and power drive our decisions, we're destined to be like so many other species on Earth who are struggling for survival. Only we will have done it to ourselves.

Spotlight on Climate Change-makers

Xiuhtezcatl Martinez (born 2000) is an activist who defends the voice of young people in our current climate crisis. He's spoken at the United Nations, uses music to inspire change, and authored the books *We Rise* and *Imaginary Borders*. He's been a plaintiff in a lawsuit, along with other young people, against the fossil fuel industry and the federal government because he believes they're not doing enough about the climate crisis to protect future generations.

Spotlight on Climate Change-makers

Hindou Oumarou Ibrahim (born 1984) is an activist who advocates for women and indigenous cultures and how their lives are impacted by the climate crisis. For example, Lake Chad provides water to people living in countries such as Chad, Cameroon, Niger, and Nigeria, and it has shrunk by 90% since the 1960s as temperatures increase in central Africa. Ibrahim has advocated for human rights at the United Nations, at the world's Paris Climate Agreement, and at the World Economic Forum.

Chapter 10

The Clarity of 2020:

A Lesson in Looking at the Big Picture

There's an expression that hindsight is 20/20, which means that it's easier to look back on previous events with clear or sharp vision than it is to see the future. This expression took on a whole new meaning when it came to the year 2020. Looking back, the year gave us many lessons, including a new understanding of humans' vulnerabilities.

2020 began with headlines about Australian wildfires that ended up leaving an estimated 46 million acres burned and 2.46 billion reptiles, 143 million mammals, 51 million frogs, and 180 million birds either dead, injured, or displaced from their habitats. Then, news went around the world on

February 9, 2020, when scientists documented a record high temperature of 69.3°F on Seymour Island in the Antarctic Peninsula. February is one of the summer months in Antarctica, but the average temperature on Seymour Island is 33.8°F in the summer and -5.8°F in the winter.

Gospers Mountain bushfires in December of 2019, Australian wildfires were not considered extinguished or contained until March of 2020

Then, the headlines changed across the world. In February and March of 2020, billions of *Homo sapiens* completely altered their behavior due to a deadly new virus, SARS-CoV-2, a form of coronavirus. The disease from this virus is called Covid-19, which stands for "coronavirus disease 2019." This new form of the coronavirus was reported to the World Health Organization on December 31, 2019; by March the virus had spread worldwide, and the WHO declared a pandemic. The virus quickly traveled from town to town, country to country, and continent to continent, demonstrating how quickly transmission can occur in Earth's New Pangaea. Viruses themselves can't travel; they do so only by being transmitted from one host to another. But humans now travel so

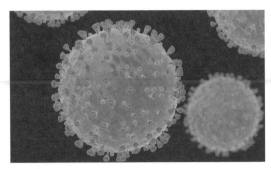

COVID-19 CORONAVIRUS particle

easily that within months, world-wide, over 75 million humans were infected and over 1.5 million people died from the virus or complications that it caused to their health.

To avoid the virus's spread, people were encouraged to wear masks that covered their mouth and nose, social distance, self-isolate, and quarantine in their homes. To keep people safe, businesses and schools closed, forcing people to work and learn from home. Events from proms to graduations were cancelled or held virtually. The summer Olympics, which were to be held in Tokyo, Japan, were postponed. The health, economic, and social costs of this pandemic were devastating.

As the events of the year unfolded, parallels to the climate crisis became apparent. Looking back on 2020 can highlight the importance of understanding the systems and feedback cycles that make large-scale problems complex to solve. Just as reducing travel and closing workplaces were not enough to contain the pandemic, we learned that just cutting back CO_2 emissions from transportation and energy use will not be enough to reverse our climate crisis.

When the pandemic began and people were staying home, climate watchers hoped for a reduction in the atmosphere's CO_2 levels, which are measured in parts per million. A dip was anticipated because in China, emissions were reduced by 25% at the start of 2020. This trend of reduced emissions spread around the world with the virus.

In April of 2020, the United States emissions of CO_2 were 16% lower than in April of 2019. With so many businesses and schools closed, electricity generation was also 7%

lower in the United States. Gasoline and jet fuel use also hit record lows because people were staying home and travel was limited. Normally, transport makes up 23% of humans' emissions, 72% of that from driving and 11% from airplanes. But in 2020, for recreational purposes and to avoid potentially crowded public transportation, biking gained popularity. Some cities took initiatives to help support this shift, such as Oakland, California, where 74 miles of streets were made car-free to help encourage more biking and walking. During shutdowns from the pandemic, streets in cities like Los Angeles and London that were normally gridlocked with traffic noticed significantly reduced numbers of vehicles on the road. Covid-19 also allowed businesses to see the potential for employees to work from home even in the future beyond the virus.

As travel dropped and some people began to think that we could change some of our habits in the long term, we became aware of environmental gains. Among these were improvements in air quality in some regions. According to the World Health Organization, air pollution kills 4.2 million people a year, with 1.1 million of those deaths occurring in China. One of the factors measured in air pollution is PM2.5, which refers to the atmospheric particulate matter (PM) with a diameter of less than 2.5 micrometers, or about 3% of the diameter of a human hair. In China, cities in lockdown reduced their PM2.5 by 14.07 μgm (14.07millionths of a gram per cubic meter of air). During lockdown, the days in China defined as having "good quality air" increased by 11.4% compared to data from a year earlier. India has 14 out of the 20 most hazardous cities in the world in terms of air quality. During lockdown, in April of 2020, particle pollution decreased by 60% with a PM2.5 of 35 in New Delhi, a city of 19 million people. People in New Delhi could even see the far-off Himalayas because of the clear skies. During this time, air quality levels were labeled "satisfactory," in contrast to their usual ratings of "poor" or "very poor." Doctors in highly polluted areas reported patients with lung illnesses proclaiming how much improvement they felt with their breathing and overall health.

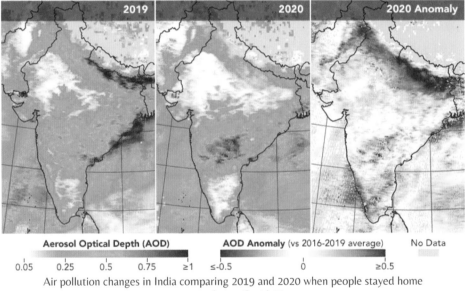

Air pollution changes in India comparing 2019 and 2020 when people stayed home more due to Covid-19

While clear environmental gains came from people staying home, the public and political focus on Covid-19 also brought opportunities for some to hurt the environment. In Brazil, illegal loggers and miners cut down 464 square miles of rainforest between January and April 2020 to create land for cattle ranchers. They did this illegally, cutting 55% more land than the year before over that same time period because the government was focused on the pandemic and was unaware of their illegal activity.

In other countries, it was the government itself that reduced environmental regulation. In the United States, the Environmental Protection Agency (EPA) proposed reducing regulations around the Clean Air Act by changing its cost-benefit formula. Restrictions around some protected conservation areas were also loosened to help local economies. President Trump signed an executive order that took away an environmental review for projects like construction of highways and pipelines carrying fossil fuels. These acts were done in the name of economic recovery, yet removing or reducing restrictions can have long-term consequences for both the environment and the economy.

Despite environmental gains made from reduced fossil fuel use during the pandemic in 2020, those gains literally went up in smoke. If you remember back to the deforestation chapter, trees capture and store carbon. When trees burn, CO_2 is released back into the atmosphere. One of the major reasons why a dip wasn't seen in the parts per million concentration of the atmosphere's CO_2 in 2020 is because there were so many long-lasting and destructive wildfires. For example, fires in the Arctic in June of 2020 released 50 million metric tons of CO_2—which is more CO_2 emissions than some countries produce in a typical year. In 2020, there were also major wildfires in Brazil, Indonesia, Argentina, Australia, and the United States. The fires in

Australia alone released almost a billion tons of CO_2.

In a given year, all humans combined emit approximately 32.5 billion metric tons of CO_2 from energy use. The fires offset gains from reduced emissions. For this reason, the conversation about climate change can't just be about human-led emissions. It has to involve a bigger picture that includes all of the systems in place that involve greenhouse gases. Some of these wildfires were started by humans, but not all, and fires, regardless of cause, are propelled by droughts. Droughts are currently longer lasting and more widespread due to warmer temperatures. Droughts affect agriculture, which impacts food production, which impacts humans' health and the economy. The economy impacts employment, which impacts the housing market, schools, and taxes. Droughts also impact surface water and groundwater levels, which ecologically can change the flow of rivers and lead to a reduction in reservoirs, which endangers the amount of water for animals and plants. When plants die, many animals lose their food source. When animals leave their home to search for food, biodiversity is impacted. Everything is connected. Learning to examine the systems in place that tend to perpetuate a problem can help people understand how to solve a problem.

Everything was also connected when it came to Covid-19, ranging from the availability of medical tests for Covid-19 to children not being able to attend school in person to the willingness or unwillingness of people to wear masks to keeping products such as toilet paper available in the grocery store. Problems like the spread of Covid-19 and the climate crisis are complicated because they involve lots of stakeholders. Stakeholders are those with an interest in the outcome of a problem or situation. When it comes to a pandemic and the changing climate, everyone is a stakeholder. Because problems are complex, it's important to have leaders who understand the systems in place and look for leverage points, which are impact areas or opportunities, to find solutions.

Perhaps the biggest lesson of 2020 comes from how individuals and leaders responded to the virus. Just as so many have ignored or denied the scientific evidence of climate change, the same wishful thinking happened with Covid-19. As a result, the states and countries that disregarded the evidence and ignored safety precautions, had higher levels than necessary of sickness and deaths, and longer periods of time before schools and businesses could re-open. Towns, cities, states, and countries that followed the scientific recommendations of mask-wearing, social distancing, and widespread testing had a safer and smoother recovery. A common term used during the pandemic was to "flatten the curve," which meant to slow down or stop the number of infection cases from continuing upward, at least long enough to allow hospitals and health care workers to catch up. When it comes to carbon emissions, we also need to stop our upward trajectory and "flatten the curve" while we learn new ways to combat the climate crisis.

Much as with climate change, those who didn't listen to the evidence about Covid-19 impacted those who did. Like invasive species, viruses know no borders. While some

Total Cases

(Linear Scale)

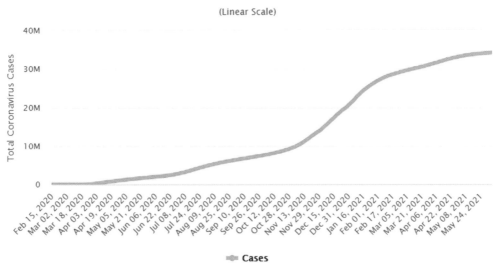

Cases

Total Coronavirus cases in the U.S.

areas had the virus under control, they were susceptible to people from elsewhere. As a result, some countries chose to limit who could and couldn't travel into their country. Closing borders and reducing the amount of travel readjusted our New Pangaea by creating geographic isolation, which slowed the virus's spread. Yet, until a vaccine was found everyone was vulnerable to the virus.

A vaccine was found in record time because resources and money were re-prioritized for this global crisis. However, when it comes to the climate crisis, there is no vaccine—no shot in the arm that can fix our changing atmosphere, altered habitats, and increasing species extinction rate. We must face what's happening and, once again, choose to change our priorities and move toward solutions-based thinking. There are similarities between Covid-19 and the climate crisis, but there are also differences.

Earth's atmosphere doesn't have borders that can be closed. Every organism shares the atmosphere, and all species are affected by it, regardless of where they live. Some individuals and countries are doing far more than others to reduce CO_2 concentrations in the atmosphere, yet we're all in this together. Like climate change, once the Covid-19 virus became widespread, it was too late to go back and make wiser decisions to change the course humans were on. Instead, we learned and adjusted. What eventually helped lessen the virus's spread were believing the evidence that masks and social distancing reduced transmission, along with supporting the scientific research, communication, and collaboration to create and administer vaccines.

We need to learn from Covid-19 and realize that priorities and habits can change when it's necessary for survival. And the evidence around climate change shows that it's critical for our species to reprioritize. The pandemic taught us that there were so many things in life, from being able to go to school to visiting loved ones, that we took for granted. As our atmosphere and its habitats and species continue to change, we will also realize that we're taking our planet for granted. We don't want to find ourselves saying, "I wish" or "I regret." Instead, this is the time for action.

Spotlight on Climate Change-makers

Michael Jarvis (born 1966) is a virologist who's developing an Ebola vaccine for gorillas. It has been estimated that up to one third of the global Western lowland gorilla population may have died due to Ebola outbreaks. Ebola can lead to internal bleeding, a high fever, vomiting, and diarrhea. The virus also impacts other species, such as humans, and spreads easily through bodily fluids. A few drops of this vaccine could potentially protect gorillas from the Ebola virus and slow down the virus's spread, helping both gorillas and humans alike.

Spotlight on Climate Change-makers

Joyce Longcore (born 1938) is a mycologist, someone who studies fungi, at the University of Maine who is one of the world's leading experts on the fungus Bd, *Batrachochytrium dendrobatidis*. Bd is the cause of an amphibian pandemic that's putting countless species of frogs in danger of going extinct. Longcore's background in studying chytrid fungi enabled her to grow Bd in pure culture and furnish her methods and cultures to researchers around the world.

* * * * * *

For better or worse, we're in this together. All of our choices matter. The final section of this book is about *your* decisions and *your* role in what happens now and in the future. The next section isn't written as a checklist of changes for you to make. Instead, look at it as a big menu of ideas; pick and choose what feels right to you. There are billions of people on this planet. The more we choose, the more positive change we will make. And the more changes we all make, the more hope we have for the future.

Part 3

Actions Speak Louder than Words:
How You Can Help

Our understanding
of Earth's history has built up
much like rocks do... slowly over time.
Our awareness of our planet, its species,
and humans' impact continues to take shape.
Layers reveal evolving history, science, politics
and clarity. We connect the dots one by one as
actions overcome fear. We choose solutions
for our planet, its habitats, and its species.

Chapter 11

What You Buy:

Changing Your Consumer Behavior

D id you know that it takes over 1,000 gallons of water to make one cotton T-shirt? Picture this T-shirt's journey, beginning in a cotton field where it's grown with or without pesticides. It then travels to a factory, most likely in Asia, where machines separate the seeds and chaff. Energy is used as the cotton fibers are then spun, combed, blended, and eventually woven into fabric on a loom. Fabric is treated with chemicals when it's bleached or dyed. It then travels to the sewing shop. On average, 15% of the fabric is wasted in the making of clothing. It's then packaged with a combination of plastic and cardboard. It travels thousands of miles by sea, land, or air.

It eventually ends up at the store, 5K race, summer camp, or wherever you get it. It then travels to your home, where it's most likely placed in a drawer with your other T-shirts.

Clothing being made

The same journey can be traced for everything we own. Imagine a child's birthday party where every guest leaves with a bag full of party favors. These bags are often filled with little plastic toys that are cheap to buy, but cost much more in the long run due to environmental damage. These low-priced toys often break easily and are played with for a few moments,

Plastic party favors

then put aside. The problem is that they never truly go away because they're often made with plastic that can't be recycled. Imagine the fossil fuels and long-lasting CO_2 emissions used in the making and transport of these toys and the centuries that the toys will exist in a landfill, in oceans, or inside an animal.

Homo sapiens own a lot of stuff. Often we don't realize the environmental impacts of these objects. There is a direct link between what you buy and your carbon footprint, which is the amount of greenhouse gas emissions that come from your choices and activities. With minimal effort, you can reduce your carbon footprint by what you do or do not purchase. When you think you need to buy something, first ask yourself a few questions. Do you really need it? How long will you use it? Could you borrow it or purchase it used?

A used soccer ball works just as well as a new soccer ball. It will save you money, and it will reduce CO_2 emissions. If you need to purchase something, first look at yard sales, thrift shops, flea markets, used sporting goods stores, or online selling communities. These are a win-win-win; you save money, the person selling the items makes money, and the atmosphere benefits.

A yard sale

If something is broken, make an effort to try and fix it. If you can't, there are repair shops that do everything from resoling shoes to fixing broken wiring in lamps. Also, maintain what you have so it will last. Washing clothes inside out helps reduce fading and will allow you to wear them longer. Washing clothes in cold water uses less energy and also reduces fading. Some clothes like jeans don't need to be washed every time you wear them. According to the Levis company, which has made jeans since 1863, you can wear jeans at least ten times before washing and they add, "Go even longer and wear them until they smell a little funky. Use a damp cloth or old toothbrush with mild soap to remove small stains instead of washing them. You know the distinct lines and creases you see on your jeans, the ones specific to you? That unique look comes from wearing your jeans for long periods without washing."

If you do need to buy something new, take the time to research what product is right for you. For example, items that need to be dry-cleaned take more energy and often use chemicals in the dry cleaning process. It's also important to know the belief of companies in regards to climate change. Some use more ecologically sound products, sell products that are made locally, and make efforts to reduce their carbon footprint. Some companies pay to have carbon offsetting of their products. This means they give money to organizations to plant trees or invest in renewable energy to offset the carbon emissions that occur in the making and selling of their products. Many companies have become carbon neutral, which means they have completely offset their greenhouse emissions to the atmosphere.

Shopping with these companies encourages them to continue being environmentally friendly. When enough consumers shop this way, it could inspire other businesses to also go carbon neutral. Many companies use labels proudly, showing they sell products made locally or in the country you live in. This is not only environmentally friendly because items don't have to be transported as far, but it helps your local economy by creating jobs. When you make a purchase, only take a paper receipt if you need one. Receipts come from trees and often have high levels of BPA. Often receipts are printed on thermal paper, which can't be recycled.

There are also choices about what is more or less sustainable in what you purchase. For example, when choosing something like wood flooring for your home, there are reclaimed flooring options or wood sources that grow back quicker than others. Clothing can also be more or less sustainable. Fashion accounts for almost 10% of humans' carbon emissions. There is something called "fast fashion," which is when clothes that are considered trendy styles are quickly moved from the runway to the stores. In the past, there were four seasons in clothing stores; now depending on the store, there are currently up to 24 seasons of clothing available each year. As a result, people are purchasing more clothes, but they are also not keeping them for as long because styles go out of fashion when there is always a new trend waiting. This is creating clothing waste both in unused clothing in people's closets and a surplus of what is no longer being sold in the stores.

Getting organized can help you see what you own, so you don't buy things unnecessarily. Looking at what you own, you may realize that you have items that you don't need. You could donate these items or organize a yard sale. Clothing or book swaps with friends is another great way to reduce your carbon footprint while getting items that are new to you. There is also a trend in having downsizing parties, where items are put out and offered to friends and families to take as gifts; this is particularly popular with people moving into a smaller home.

And if you do purchase or make a gift for someone, think about how you give it. Wrapping paper comes from trees; it has to be processed, transported, packaged, and more than half of it ends up in the trash. Rather than using store-bought wrapping paper, you could give the gift in a reusable bag, wrap

A gift wrapped in fabric

it in a page of newspaper comics, or wrap it with a cloth napkin and ribbon—which could then be reused.

Start to think about the true environmental cost of the things you own and what you buy. Become mindful of what materials were used, how long you'll keep it, and what greenhouse emissions went into making, packaging, and transporting it. Remember that everything you purchase has an impact.

Chapter 12

What You Eat:

The Green Plate

J ust as the items you purchase for yourself have an environmental impact, so does the food that you eat. This impact can be seen by how food is grown— in terms of water use, land use, chemical use—how far it travels, and how much of the food you waste. Depending on what you eat, food accounts for 10-30% of each household's carbon footprint.

The most significant impact on our greenhouse gas emissions around food is our decision about what to eat. Because meat involves the birth and growth of an animal, which consumes resources, followed by the processing and packaging of that animal's meat, producing meat uses more

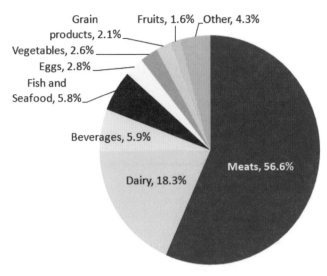

Grain products, 2.1%
Fruits, 1.6%
Other, 4.3%
Vegetables, 2.6%
Eggs, 2.8%
Fish and Seafood, 5.8%
Beverages, 5.9%
Dairy, 18.3%
Meats, 56.6%

Greenhouse gas contributions of an average diet

energy than producing fruit, vegetables, or grains. Grazing animals are also a primary source of methane emissions, which is a greenhouse gas that is effective at holding heat. Methane can be 28 times stronger over a 100-year time period than CO_2 at causing temperatures to rise and 80 times stronger over a 20-year period. In particular, beef and dairy cattle release high quantities of methane because they burp and fart so much; one cow releases approximately a gallon of methane every 30 minutes. This comes out to 150 to 250 pounds of methane a year from one cow. There are currently over a billion cows that are used for meat or dairy consumption.

In addition to methane, CO_2 is another greenhouse gas that has increased emissions due to meat consumption. One meal size serving of beef averages out to about 6.61

pounds of CO_2 emissions, while one serving of pork is 1.72 pounds, and a serving of poultry is 1.26 pounds. Comparatively, one serving of rice averages out to 0.16 pounds of CO_2 emissions, while one serving of carrots averages out to 0.07 pounds.

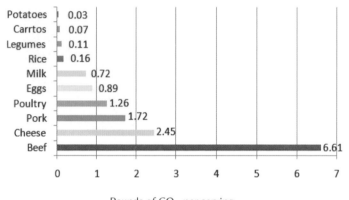

Pounds of CO_2 per serving
(4 oz. meat, 1/2 cup asparagus & carrots, 8 oz. liquids)

The food we eat is also linked to water usage because the growth of everything, ranging from meat to grains to produce, requires water. Meat requires significantly more water because so much is used to grow the food that the animal eats. Then the animal themselves need to drink water. Depending on its size, a cow, for example, will drink between 3 and 30 gallons of water a day. On average, it takes 1,840 gallons of water to yield one pound of beef. This can be compared to 180 gallons of water for one pound of wheat and 100 gallons of water for one pound of potatoes. Therefore, 18.4 pounds of potatoes are equal to one pound of beef in terms of water usage.

The products of animals, such as milk and cheese, also

have high greenhouse emissions. One serving of cheese from cow's milk averages out to 2.45 pounds of CO_2 emissions. The same amounts of cow's milk, almond milk, soymilk, and oat milk all have significantly different greenhouse gases emissions. One serving of cow's milk equals 1.3 pounds of CO_2 emissions, while almond milk is 0.3 pounds, soymilk is 0.43 pounds, and oat milk is 0.4 pounds. To give a comparison, the average car driven emits 0.9 pounds of CO_2 per mile.

However, the water usage for milk types, including those that are vegan, can be surprising. It requires 312 cups of water to make one glass (200ml) of almond milk. The same amount of rice milk uses 228 cups of water. One glass of cow's milk requires over 500 cups of water. Overall, cow's milk requires far more water, land usage, and greenhouse gas emissions than milk that doesn't come from animals. It's important to understand the amount of energy, and often waste, that goes into what we drink and eat.

Carbon emissions from seafood don't depend primarily on land or water usage; instead, 90% of the carbon emissions come from fuel used to catch and transport seafood. It's estimated that 80% to 90% of the world's fishing stock is overexploited or fully exploited. Some of the most common seafood eaten includes cod, haddock, tuna, salmon, and shrimp. Adding variety to what seafood people eat can also help the overall sustainability of seafood, which will also help biodiversity.

It's also important to know how the seafood you eat has been caught, because some fishing methods have more negative consequences than others. Explosives are used with dynamite fishing, or blast fishing, to stun or kill fish. In the process, the fish's habitat, especially when it's a coral reef, can be destroyed. Unnecessary death also happens due to bycatch. Bycatch is the name of unwanted species caught along with the desired species in fishing nets. Often bycatch are thrown back into the ocean dead. But some restaurants are cooking bycatch to show that they also have value. However, not all bycatch can be used for food. Dolphins, whales, seabirds and sea turtles are often unintentionally caught in drift gillnets, which are a wall of netting that hangs vertically. Once tangled, the animals either get injured or drown.

Buying locally harvested seafood will help your local economy and have a lower carbon footprint. The distance that food travels is a key component to making decisions about food. Take, for example, a kiwi fruit that's grown in New Zealand. For those who live in New Zealand, this is a locally grown food. But if you live anywhere else in the world, that kiwi would have to travel thousands, possibly over 10,000 miles, to get to you. A kiwi is a small fruit that is eaten quickly, but its travel impact stays in the atmosphere much longer. The average distance that conventionally-grown food travels to the grocery store is 1,494 miles. Choosing locally grown produce or meat instead has a significantly lower carbon footprint. For example, a research study found that food grown in the state of Iowa that was sold locally travelled on average 56 miles.

Going to a local farmers' market or farm stands reduces the distance that food is traveling and supports the local economy. Food from farmers' markets is also fresher because it doesn't have to be picked as far in advance. For example, apples are picked in the fall, so when you go to the grocery store and buy one in the summer, it's either been shipped from far away or has been in storage for months. To allow produce to be stored for months, many companies slow the ripening process by filling storage containers or food packaging with nitrogen gas. For some produce, they then use chemicals when it's time for ripening to begin. This happens to bananas, which are the most popular fruit in the world, with over 100 billion eaten each year. The majority of the world's bananas come from Central America, South America, Africa, and Asia. Producers pick bananas when they are green, then store them in a ventilated room. When the sellers are ready for them to ripen, they pump ethylene gas into the room—the gas that bananas naturally emit to ripen. The gas is then removed from the room because the

Bananas after harvest

bananas have been given the signal that they should start to ripen. When yellowing begins, they start their shipping route to stores, knowing that they will continue to ripen on their journey. A benefit of this process is that it cuts down on food waste, but a downside is that food is altered.

Farmers' markets allow you to get fresher, less scientifically modified food. At farmer's markets you won't get the same variety of food as at grocery stores. You won't be able to buy strawberries on a snowy day in the middle of winter, because the produce at farmer's markets is grown locally. At the same time, you won't be paying to transport packaged strawberries hundreds or thousands of miles.

A farmer's market

To support local farms, many farms sell farm shares, or CSAs—Community Supported Agriculture—where you invest in a farm and get a portion of what is harvested each year to eat. Or you could plant your own garden and could cut down on your carbon emissions by not needing to travel to buy produce as often.

Buying food from farmers or growing your own also significantly reduces packaging. According to the Environmental Protection Agency, in 2017, 80.1 million tons of waste came from packaging and containers. Even at grocery stores you can reduce packaging by buying loose, unpackaged produce and by using your own bags at checkout. How about when you go to a restaurant? If you think you'll have extra food to take home, you can bring your own storage containers with you. This cuts down on trash and recycling, and also can help your health. Most takeaway containers are made with plastic, paper, or Styrofoam that should not be microwaved, because they can leach out toxic chemicals. And if you buy takeout food, be sure to tell the seller that you don't need plastic utensils.

Another way to reduce food packaging is to drink water in your own water bottle. It's estimated that over one million plastic water bottles are purchased each minute around the globe. While the country of Norway recycles 97% of plastic bottles, the United State recycles only 30%. Even when plastic is recycled it gets weaker, so rather than becoming what it was before, it becomes a different form of plastic, often of lower quality; this is called downcycling. An estimated 60 million plastic bottles end up at landfills each day, which comes out to almost 22 billion plastic bottles thrown away a year. Not only will the bottles last for centuries, but resources were used to make the bottles, and the greenhouse emissions have an on-going impact. Five hundred billion disposable cups are also used every year; using your own travel mug cuts down on waste and emissions. But don't buy too many water bottles or travel mugs, even reusable ones, because in order to make and sell these products, resources were used and greenhouse gases emitted.

For items in your travel mug, such as coffee, there are also better choices about what you buy. One of the world's biggest exporters of coffee is Brazil, which is where the Amazon rainforest is located. Farmers often clear-cut trees so they can grow coffee. Contrary to what you would think, even though the rainforest is so lush and green, the soil is not great for growing crops. The soil itself lacks nutrients; the majority of the nutrients are stored in the trees and plants. The poor soil means that farmers keep moving to new land, cutting down more trees to try to grow more crops. One coffee-farming method that helps reduce deforestation is called shade-grown coffee. This is when some of the trees are left standing and coffee plants grow under the canopy of the trees. This arrangement helps nutrients stay

Shade grown coffee

in the soil, which yields a better crop and reduces the need to cut or burn down more trees. Having access to trees also helps migratory birds and butterflies. Coffee grown in this more sustainable way will have a label on the bag that says "shade-grown" or "bird-friendly." When consumers buy these products, it shows companies the value people put on purchasing food that is grown and harvested in more environmentally friendly ways.

Birds, butterflies, bees, bats, beetles, and other insects have an important role for humans and the food that we eat, because they are pollinators. Pollinators are essential to agriculture because they move pollen from the male portion of flowers, the anthers, to the female portion, the stigma. Pollinators fertilize plants as they travel from flower to flower looking for nectar; in the process the pollen brushes onto them and they become a delivery service for plant reproduction. It's estimated that one out of every three bites of food we eat is pollinated. Due to loss of their natural habitat

Bees are an essential pollinator

and pesticide use, pollinators are struggling, and their populations have been dropping drastically. The rusty patched bumblebee was listed under the Endangered Species Act in 2017. To help pollinators, you can plant native species that pollinators need, such as milkweed, black-eyed Susans, pale purple coneflowers, and fruit-bearing bushes or trees. Pollinators also love dandelions. Many people think of these as weeds, but they are an important food source for pollinators—rather than mowing them, let them grow!

The final thing you can do is appreciate the food that you eat. Think about where your food grew and the journey that it took to get to you. Start to see the connection that your food has to Earth and the impact that your choices make.

Chapter 13

What You Throw Away:

Trash, Compost, and Recycling

It's nearly impossible to avoid waste altogether, but there are some actions you can take to reduce what ends up in the landfill. When it comes to food, the goal is to avoid food waste by only buying the amount you need. Planning out meals before you go to the grocery store can lead to less waste. Most items that aren't eaten can also be frozen for when you do need them, such as bread, cooked rice, or cookies. Even dairy products, like milk and cheese, can be frozen.

According to the Environmental Protection Agency, 20% of landfill waste is food. In the landfill, food doesn't have the air that it needs to break down—instead, it releases methane, a greenhouse gas. Landfills account for 34% of all methane emissions in the United States. Rather than throwing away food waste, composting it breaks down food scraps into nutrient-rich compost. When compost is mixed with soil it acts like a natural fertilizer and helps plants grow.

The EPA organizes compost into the following categories: *greens*—grass clippings, produce waste, and coffee grounds; *browns*—dead leaves, branches, and twigs; and *water*—which helps the organic materials break down. If compost gets hot enough, anything that grows can be composted, including dairy, meat, and bones. Many towns and cities have programs, or businesses, that give you a small bucket to put food scraps in each week and do curbside pick up at your house or apartment. The food scraps are taken for compost, and the bucket is replaced with a clean one.

Compost that is collected from homes weekly as part of a "Garbage to Garden" program

Keeping landfill waste to a minimum can reduce both methane emissions and the leaching of toxins. One challenge for landfills is that so many items that could be recycled, particularly plastic, end up in landfills instead. This waste is due to people not recycling properly and a result of

China's 2018 decision to no longer accept recycling imports. For decades, we shipped our trash and recycling problems thousands of miles away. While it may feel like a step back to have so much recycling currently end up in landfills, this could lead countries to find ways to deal with their own recycling problems. Current discussions focus on shipping our recycling to countries in Africa, but transporting plastic thousands of miles adds to its environmental impact and simply avoids the problem. The problem is that we use too much plastic and that we lack good ways to deal with recyclables. We also need to cut down on single-use plastic, ranging from plastic bags to packaging, because these plastics leach chemicals that may be harmful, endanger wildlife, and add to our planet's CO_2 emissions.

Sorting recycling

Changing the volume of trash we produce begins by shifting how we look at waste and paying attention to how much it has become a part of our daily life. Recognizing waste will help us determine how to reduce it. For example, when you check the mail, how often do you get what we call "junk mail?" Instead of thinking of it as junk mail, think about the trees that were cut down, the energy used in making it, and the fuel used in transportation. Then, after a glance, the junk mail lands right in the recycling bin—where it may or may not be recycled. One thing you can do is email companies and ask to be removed from their mailing lists. Another option is to pay a fee of two dollars, which covers you for ten years, and follow the steps on the United States Postal Service's website to remove your name from

A pile of junk mail

catalogs and other mail offers. If you want magazines, many libraries have subscriptions to a variety of titles and give away old copies for free. Or you could subscribe to a magazine, then after reading it, share it with friends.

We need to let new habits and new routines form. Bringing your own reusable bags to stores, bringing your own takeaway containers to restaurants, and saying no thank you to a plastic disposable straw at restaurants are easy lifestyle changes that add up. Other easy changes are planning ahead to avoid using disposable forks and spoons by bringing your own silverware. Instead of paper towels and napkins, use cloth towels and cloth napkins that can be easily added to laundry that you're already doing. Rather than buying soap that comes in a plastic bottle, purchase bars of soap—preferably without any packaging.

There are stores that allow you to bring in your own containers for household items and refill them. These include bringing in empty bottles for liquid hand soap, dish soap, laundry detergent, and shampoo, which often cost less per ounce to refill than you would pay in the store for new bottles of products. Often these stores have more natural products. Natural products are important because another form of waste is what goes down your drain from the cleaning products that you use. Many products contain chemicals that do harm when entering the water system, such as bisphenol and polychlorinated biphenyls (PCN).

To avoid toxins leaching, it's important to know how to properly dispose of items like paint, batteries, light bulbs, and electronics. When buying paint, all major paint brands offer low or zero VOC, Volatile Organic Compounds, paint options. VOCs cause the odor that paint lets off and can be harmful to people, pets, and the environment. When you think you're ready to throw a paint can away, first see if you can use any of the extra paint for household projects or donate it to someone else who may use it. Many states have laws allowing you to

An old paint can

drop off cans of unused paint at paint stores, regardless of whether the paint was purchased there or not. The paint stores make sure that these cans are disposed of following guidelines. States pay for this program by putting a small fee on paint cans at the time of purchase. If your state does not have this program, it should have a household hazardous waste program, which collects items like oil-based or old lead paint. If your state has neither of these programs, you should write letters to your state representative about these programs' importance. In the meantime, you can wait for such a program to exist to dispose of the paint or if you need to dispose of it now, add cat litter to the can before you throw it away to dry out the paint and help prevent the leaking of toxins.

When it comes to single-use batteries that are sizes AAA, AA, C, D, 6V and 9V made today, they don't have the same toxic materials that they had in the past. As of 1996, these batteries no longer contain mercury and are now considered safe to throw away in the trash. Larger size batteries, like car batteries, can be returned to local auto supply stores for safe disposal of hazardous material and recycling of the metal.

For light bulbs, standard incandescent lights, halogen lights, and LED lights can be disposed of in the trash. Compact fluorescent lamps (CFLs) and fluorescent tube lights contain mercury and need to be brought to a dropoff point such as at a large home improvement store or a special location at landfills. When you buy either of these styles of light bulbs, part of the purchase price includes a fee to have the bulb properly disposed of, and if possible, to have some of its parts recycled. Of these light bulbs, standard incandescent lights are the least environmentally friendly because of their energy use and how often they need to be replaced. LED and CFL lights use 75% less energy to operate. Compared to an incandescent light that lasts for 1,000 hours on average, a CFL can last 1,000 to 3,000 hours and a LED can last 25,000 hours, which leads to significantly less trash.

For electronics that no longer work, you can try to have them fixed rather than replacing them. Or you can offer them for free to others who may want to try and fix them. Some stores and websites that sell electronics will also take electronics for recycling. Depending on what the electronics are and how badly they are damaged, there are also companies that will buy them from you at a low price.

These choices will save you money, lower your carbon footprint, and reduce your waste footprint.

Chapter 14

How You Use Energy:
Heating, Cooling, Driving, and More

Have you ever had leftover lasagna from the oven, wrapped it up, and then put it in the refrigerator? This is a simple act that people do every day, but if you let that lasagna cool down to room temperature before you put it in the refrigerator, it will use less energy. The refrigerator is working hard to keep food cold; by putting food in that's hot, you force the refrigerator to work harder to cool it down. When it doesn't have to work so hard, the refrigerator uses less energy. Room by room in your house, there are easy ways to reduce your carbon footprint.

Three of your most energy-using appliances in your house are the refrigerator, washing machine, and dryer. For all appliances, try to have energy star rated appliances that use less energy, and therefore save you money and reduce green-house emissions. To save energy when doing laundry, make sure you have a full load of laundry

The Energy Star logo

washed in cold water and put the washing machine on the highest spin cycle to remove excess water. If you need to use the dryer, having more water spun from the clothes will help them dry faster and will use less electricity. Hanging your clothes to dry saves a lot of money and greenhouse gas emissions. Rather than using electricity or natural gas to heat your dryer to 125-135°F, you can let the Sun's warmth dry your clothes for free. Even starting with something like

Towels hung out to dry

drying towels in the Sun rather than the dryer will make a difference. Towels take up a lot of room in the dryer that could be saved for other clothes, and they hang easily and dry quickly.

In the bathroom, the goal is to reduce water and heat waste. To save gallons of water each day, use a low-flow showerhead and low-flush toilet. On average, people tend to use less water by showering than taking baths. For example, an eight-minute shower uses about 17 gallons of water, whereas filling an average size 70-gallon bathtub a third of the way full uses 23.3 gallons of water. Heating the water for baths and showers uses energy. For a shower, don't leave the room as the water is warming up. On average, 20% of the time that showers are running, nobody is in them. This wastes 2 to 2.5 gallons of water a minute. Stand by the shower, and as soon as it's the temperature you'd like, get in. Some tips to take shorter showers are to set an alarm for a goal amount of time like five minutes. Another tip is to take some tasks out of showering. Some people brush their teeth in the shower; this uses far more water than the sink. When standing at the sink, it's also easy to turn the water off when you're brushing your teeth.

In your living room, energy use depends on the season. Let's imagine it's warm outside. When you're not in a room, turning off lights and closing the shades helps keep it cooler. An electric fan in the room that you're in uses much less energy than an air conditioner that cools the entire space. The same is true in the winter. If you're cold, rather than turning up the whole house's heat, put a sweater or blanket on. In your living room, you may also have a television. Turn the TV off when you're not watching it. Most TVs also have settings which allow you to turn down the brightness or backlighting on the TV, thereby using less energy. If you can, watch shows or movies on a laptop or tablet, both of which use less energy than a full-sized television.

There are also businesses that will do energy audits for your house, giving advice and cost estimates on everything from new energy-efficient windows to reducing air leaks to adding insulation. Insulation placed in attics or between the outside and inside walls of a house creates a barrier that cuts down on heat loss. The investment in insulation can help reduce energy bills. Often, tax rebates are given to offset the cost.

Your home's size is one of the biggest indicators of carbon footprint because it impacts how much stuff you own and how much energy you use. Your energy source also matters; for example, many homes are heated by oil, coal, or natural gas, which are fossil fuels. These are nonrenewable, meaning they will eventually run out, and they all release greenhouse gas emissions. Having clean energy like solar panels can significantly lower your carbon emissions. Solar is considered clean energy because it comes from a renewable source, the Sun, and leads to no greenhouse emissions, except for what occurred when the panels were made and transported to your house. This form of energy works when sunlight activates the solar panels' solar cells, or photovoltaic cells, and they produce an electrical current. This electricity can be used to operate anything needing electricity, including appliances and heating and cooling systems. If you don't have enough sunlight or money for solar panels on your home, or if you rent property rather than own, there are other options such as joining a community solar farm. For these, you buy or rent into community solar panels, which credit your electricity bill with your portion of the kilowatt hours that are harvested from the panels. If you move, you can take your credits with you.

Solar panels

Your yard also has a great impact. According to the Environmental Protection Agency, using a lawn mower for one hour is the equivalent in emissions as driving an average sized car 350 miles. Seventeen million gallons of gas are also spilled each year when people add gas to the lawnmower's tank. Mow-free yards are becoming more and more popular. Creating such a yard involves steps like planting more trees, converting grass to gardens, and planting low-growing grasses and shrubbery. If you do choose to mow, keeping your lawn at a height of 2.5 to 3 inches will prevent you from needing to use fertilizers to stimulate growth. If you do need fertilizers, compost is more natural than artificial, chemical-based fertilizers. Instead of chemical pesticides, natural alternatives can be used depending on the need, such as vinegar. A goal is to avoid fertilizers and pesticides from getting into the groundwater, which can impact other species. If you do choose to use these products, it's important to not use them before rain or watering your lawn. Otherwise, the chemicals mix with water and wash away to other habitats, causing unintended consequences. If you water your lawn, there are smart watering systems that connect online to weather forecasts which will determine if lawn watering should or should not be done that day. And finally, if you can, plant trees. Lots and lots of trees. Trees absorb CO_2 and create food sources and homes for animals.

Rain Skip

353 Gallons Saved*

Weather Intelligence applied a Rain Skip for Every Day (Rachio-EB4AB8) at 05:02 AM

It's raining today, no watering needed

top: Grass being watering with automatic sprinklers even when it's raining

left: A reading from a smart watering system indicating that it did not turn on sprinklers due to the rain

When leaving your house, the choices you make also impact your carbon footprint. Choices like walking, riding a bike, taking public transportation, and carpooling add up, especially when lots of people make these choices. Every time you take the bus to school instead of being dropped off in a car, you reduce greenhouse emissions.

Using a bike as a family vehicle rather than a car

The car that you drive also has varying emissions depending on how old it is, its size, and its energy source. Fuel efficiency refers to how much energy a vehicle can get from fuel, often measured in miles per gallon. Some environmentally friendly car choices are hybrids, which have an electric motor and a gasoline engine, and electric cars that use no gas. Electric cars are particularly good when the electricity comes from renewable sources, like solar or wind energy.

These methods will all save money by lowering your energy bills while at the same time you reduce your carbon footprint.

Chapter 15

How You Vote:

Electing Leaders Who Lead Us in the Right Direction

W hen it comes to large-scale changes, politicians make decisions that impact all of us. Individuals' actions make a difference, but the simple act of voting for the right leaders will lead to the most significant change.

Policy is the course of action taken by leadership. The laws that people attempt to pass or enact are called legislation. New policy and laws are what will change the dangerous and destructive path that we're on. One of the best examples of legislation that made a significant difference is the Endangered Species Act, passed by Congress in 1974. It has saved countless animals' habitats and brought many species back from near extinction, including the bald eagle, which is no longer endangered. The Clean Air and Clean Water Acts of 1963 and 1972 reduced pollution by holding individuals and companies accountable for their actions. These acts, which passed after Rachel Carson published *Silent Spring* in 1962 and as the environmental movement was getting underway, are still some of the strongest environmental policies in place in the United States.

An example of the world coming together for positive change is the way countries of the world handled CFCs, or chlorofluorocarbons. In 1974, scientists discovered that CFCs had a negative impact on the ozone layer, and ten years of research supported these findings. CFCs are manufactured chemicals that were common in aerosol cans, food packaging, refrigerators, and air conditioners. After the emitted CFCs entered the atmosphere, they reacted chemically, which led to Earth's ozone layer thinning and breaking down. The ozone layer protects us from ultraviolet (UV light), which can cause skin cancers and a clouding of the eye's lens, a condition called cataracts. Release of CFCs created an ozone hole over Antarctica, and it was gradually expanding to populated areas of the Southern Hemisphere.

In 1987, countries came together and negotiated the Montreal protocol, which led most countries to ban CFCs by the 1990s, with the rest of the world following in 2010. Current NASA data shows that CFC bans and regulations are making a difference. The ban has caused chlorine levels to go down in the atmosphere, allowing the ozone layer to slowly recover. Earth is resilient when we give it the ability to recover from our damage.

Another example of worldwide collaboration is the 2015 Paris Agreement, in which nations came together to respond to the threat of climate change. The agreement they reached called for countries to track and report on their emissions, make efforts to limit a global temperature increase, and work to reduce their emissions. On Earth Day, April 22nd, 2016, commitments and agreements were signed by 175 countries, including the three countries that emit the most greenhouse gases: China, India, and the United States. The Paris Agreement was signed under President Obama's leadership. In June of 2017, President Trump announced that the United States would withdraw from the international agreement because it would harm the United States' economy. In 2021, one of President Biden's first acts as president was to reinstate the United States' commitment to every clause and article of the agreement. The values and priorities of politicians are reflected by the policies they do or do not support.

Who we elect as leaders, and the laws they pass, can have a long-lasting and far-stretching impact. This is true on both a local and national level. In the United States, California consistently sets the standard by passing their own state legislation. California's rules far exceed the federal environmental standards passed by the United States Congress. California's more rigorous standards apply to everything from fuel efficiency to chemicals used on furniture and in food packaging. Because California has such a large population, over 39 million people, many companies build their products to meet California's strict standards and sell them nationwide. As a result, the government in one state can have a positive impact nationwide.

Who we elect will also impact the industries and individuals that politicians choose to receive tax breaks and other incentives. As shown in chapter 9, some politicians have prioritized support for the fossil fuel industry, while others have focused on renewable energy. What would it look like if the next generation of leaders prioritize the climate crisis? What if towns, cities, and states were given financial compensation for having a high percentage of trees and plants to absorb carbon dioxide? This idea could encourage everything from rooftop gardens to planting more trees to protecting trees that are already mature. For example, Maine is the most forested state in the country, with 89% of the state being covered in trees. Imagine how it would change priorities if financial incentives were provided for the enormous value that trees provide through their absorption of CO_2.

However, the discussion of *value* is where politicians, and society as a whole, often disagree. Trees have a different value to different people. In fact, a core aspect of the climate crisis and humans' perspective of Earth comes down to the perspective from which people value Earth and its resources. People show their priorities by how they vote, and politicians show their priorities by the policies they support. Politicians also show their priorities by how they create economic strategies around commodities. This can be seen in regards to the climate crisis through the *cap and trade* approach, which had widespread implementation in the 1990s and still exists today in various countries. This method seeks to balance the economy and resources by first looking at how much of a common resource should be used by all involved in an industry. The industry is then capped, or limited, as to the total amount of resources that they can use. Resources that may be used are divided up depending on companies' size. Then, those companies that are energy efficient and use fewer resources can sell their excess allotment to other companies. Essentially, this is emissions trading; the inefficient companies get what they need and those that are more efficient get a profit.

Some view this as a great compromise between economic and environmental needs; however, others criticize the cap-and-trade model, saying it doesn't do enough. This model allows businesses that are not energy efficient to buy what they need from other companies, so not enough of a reduction occurs. Of course, this outcome depends on where the overall resource level is set, which is again influenced by politicians' priorities and values.

Many critics argue that cap-and-trade does not do enough about the actual problem, which is reducing emissions and overconsumption of natural resources. Understanding the actual problem is key to any solutions-based thinking. Problems are complex, but one method to understanding them better is by examining the root cause of the problem. Examining the root cause of a problem means digging deep to figure out what the real causes are. The deeper you delve into a problem, the more likely you are to understand the values and events that led to the problem existing. Once people understand a problem's sources, they can find solutions. Leverage points are opportunities to do something about a problem.

Many believe that the biggest leverage point to reduce our greenhouse gas emissions is to put in place a carbon tax. Taxes are financial charges to businesses or individuals which governments use to fund something important to the public. They pay for everything from roads to fire departments to public schools. All states have real estate property tax, most have sales tax, and some cities even have their own additional taxes on items like plastic bags or sugar-sweetened beverages. As these examples show, governments sometimes tax items that are unhealthy to people or the environment. For example, to encourage people not to smoke, there is a federal cigarette tax of $1.01 per pack, and some states charge over four dollars in taxes for a package of 20 cigarettes. This money often goes toward anti-smoking efforts and health care programs. Many believe this same approach should be used toward greenhouse gases by creating a carbon tax. A carbon tax would apply fees to companies and products based on fossil fuel emissions. Ideally, the tax would reflect the long-term cost of their environmental impacts.

Think back to chapter 11's example of the party bag full of cheap plastic toys that break easily and can't be recycled. How would the cost change if these plastic toys carried an added carbon tax? If the toys were no longer cheap, would people still purchase them? Just as the fee for proper disposal is added to the can of paint or LED lights when you buy them, what if a fee was put on products to offset their greenhouse emissions? This would change what consumers buy and how companies make their products. Just as food packaging already lists ingredients and nutritional facts, what if it also included environmental information such as greenhouse gases or the amount of water used to make the food? Would it change the amount of milk wasted if someone knew that to yield one glass of cow's milk, it took over 500 cups of water? How do we make the environmental impact of items we purchase transparent to customers?

Perhaps we haven't made environmental impacts easy to see because some industries or lobbyists don't want this aspect of what they are selling to be transparent. When you dig deep into why transparency isn't there, it often comes back to greed and once again *profit over planet*. Changes to our policy and priorities will only happen if we elect people who value protecting Earth's air, land, water, and species. From there, solutions will only be put in place if we elect people who understand the complexities of the problems we have created.

Earth's climate change and humans' impact on it have been researched and discussed for decades, yet too many voters and leaders do not understand the evidence showing it's happening or the ramifications of a changing atmosphere, rising global temperatures, and a more acidic ocean. In 1988, in an effort to bring science and policy together, the United Nations Intergovernmental Panel on Climate Change was formed. That was 33 years ago. The topic of climate change isn't new, but how we look at it needs to change. Instead of investing in subsidies for a fossil fuel industry that adds to our climate crisis and will eventually leave us without energy, we need to invest instead in cleaner energy.

Over a million Americans work in the fossil fuel industry. We need to promote change without abandoning them. During the Covid-19 pandemic, in the spring of 2020, the United States government gave financial support to taxpayers who had an adjusted gross income less than $75,000. Each adult below that income level received $1,200, with $500 for each child. The Covid-19 pandemic showed that we can reprioritize funding when we need to. We need to redirect subsidies toward clean energy jobs. The government can subsidize training and promote new businesses to start in communities that previously relied on income from the fossil fuel industry. We can make this change, we just have to choose to do so.

One of the biggest obstacles to any change is fear. Understandably, people are afraid of losing their jobs and not being able to support themselves and/or their families. Many politicians speak to these fears and criticize alternative energy to ensure they get votes from people working in the fossil fuel industry. Sadly, many politicians' driving force is not what's best for the people they represent in the long term, but making sure they're re-elected and stay in power. They try to stay popular by telling voters what they want to hear. This tendency is heightened when lobbyists try to influence those politicians to vote a certain way in return for the campaign money they need.

This observation brings us to the biggest questions of all. What happens when our leaders don't lead us in the right direction? The answer is simple: We need new leaders.

For this to happen, people need to vote. In the 2016 Presidential election, 40% of eligible voters, almost 100 million people, did not cast a vote. In 2020, the number of people choosing not to vote fell to 33% of people. Voting matters. What if we could inspire that last third of the country to vote for the planet's future? That's why we need

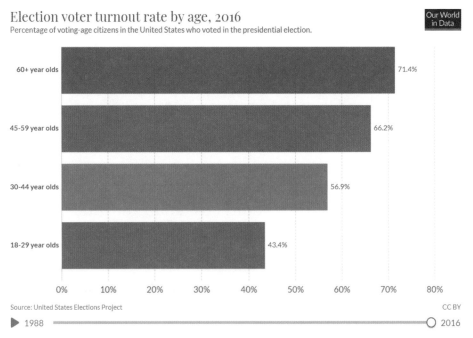

Election voter turnout rate by age, 2016
Percentage of voting-age citizens in the United States who voted in the presidential election.

Source: United States Elections Project

Less than half of 18-29 year olds voted in the 2016 U.S. presidential election people like you, who take the time to understand the issues, to advocate, communicate, and run for leadership positions. Whether you run for student council or town council or as a state representative or U.S. Senator or President, we need people who will work courageously toward solving the problems we face. We need people who don't just think about themselves in this moment, but look at the bigger picture in the long run. Climate change impacts all of us, regardless of age, income, country, or race. Resources are being depleted, species are going extinct, and Earth's oceans and atmosphere will soon be past the point of recovery.

Voting and running for office are two ways to use your voice for change; other ways are through writing and speaking. Reach out to your school board about the importance of supporting local farmers and having gardens where students help grow food. Help students understand how riding the school bus rather than having their parents drop them off reduces carbon emissions. Write or speak to your town council about the importance of making town services more energy-efficient and supporting recycling at local landfills.

When advocating for a cause, take the time to research how much these efforts would cost and how much money they can save in the long run. Write op-eds, opinion pieces, for newspapers. Write letters to politicians giving your reasons why they should support policy that reduces greenhouse emissions. Write letters to those you believe can make a difference. Olga Owens Huckins' letter to Rachel Carson about her observations of birds dying after DDT was sprayed inspired Rachel Carson to research and write the book *Silent Spring*—and that began the environmental movement.

When enough of us educate ourselves, change our actions, and use our voice to inspire others, we <u>will</u> make a difference.

Part 4

In Conclusion: We have a Choice

Our understanding
of Earth's history has built up
much like rocks do... slowly over time.
Our awareness of our planet, its species,
and humans' impact continues to take shape.
Layers reveal evolving history, science, politics
and clarity. We connect the dots one by one, as
actions overcome fear. We choose solutions
for our planet, its habitats, and its species.
Truth becomes our inspiration and
our compass guiding us
toward tomorrow.

Take a walk outside. It doesn't matter what season it is or where you live. Try to find a spot away from people and buildings and roads and just let yourself take in what you see. Maybe you're in a forested part of a park or at a beach or in a grassy field or on a mountain or in your backyard. Pay attention to the variety of sounds you hear and the animals and plants that you see. Look up at the sky and feel the Sun, or moonlight, or wind on your face. If you can, touch the soil or the snow or the sand. Let yourself think about the immensity of Earth. It's easy to forget that we're on a planet, *one of billions*, in a galaxy, *one of two trillion galaxies*, in the Universe. It's easy to forget how long this planet has been here and how many species have called it home. It's easy to forget how many species have gone extinct, while Earth has continued to re-volve around the Sun billions of times. It's easy to forget how much the air, land, and sea have changed. It's easy to forget that without words, Earth is speaking to us and con-stantly teaching us. We can choose to listen to the evidence that Earth and its species are showing us and change our actions, or we can choose to live, or not live, with the con-sequences.

Earth existed for billions of years before us and will continue to exist with or without us. This book is about understanding that species have been vulnerable throughout Earth's history. *Homo sapiens* are vulnerable too. Yet, we are unique in our ability to learn from the past, reflect on the present, and alter our own future. Through data and observations, we see the ocean acidifying and species going extinct. We understand the impact these changes will have on all marine species, including those (like us) who rely on the ocean for food. We know global temperatures are increasing, which will cause ice to melt, low-lying islands to be submerged, wildfires to increase, and droughts to come more often and last longer. We understand the impact that heat, drought, loss of land surface, and wildfires will have on food insecurity. We know that hunger will cause mass migrations of animals, including humans. Many of these organisms will have nowhere to go. There will be humans without homes or food or hope. We can predict the chaos such human misery will create and the potential for local and global conflicts to occur. We can predict a world polarized by those driven by greed and others holding onto humanity. We will shift from caring about selfies and social media or political parties or propaganda to simply survival— all a result of us changing the planet faster than we can keep up with. A changing planet is why *all* species have gone extinct.

But, we're not extinct. We are different from the trilobites, the land dinosaurs, the Neanderthals, and everything in between. They couldn't see what was coming, but we can. We understand that we have a role in what's happening to Earth's atmosphere, habitats, and species. We also understand that we have more than a role; we have a choice. And what each of us chooses matters.

With that final message, please take a breath.

Some of you took a breath to give you energy and others took a breath because you're exhausted.

For those of you who have a fire inside you to make changes to your lifestyle and to use your voice to educate and empower others... Go for it! We need you and we thank you! With full support, I encourage you to stop reading and get to it!

For those of you who feel overwhelmed by a world with so many problems and so much denial that it makes you want to SCREAM! I'm with you. You should be angry. Decisions are being made that will affect your life and your children's lives. Even worse, many people making these decisions won't be alive in 2050 when CO_2 concentrations are expected to top 500 parts per million or 2100 when our planet hits what many scientists believe is our planet's tipping point. You're inheriting a planet with problems that you didn't create. You have every right to feel angry. So, what do you do with your knowledge and your frustration?

Like any problems you face (big or small), at some point you need to decide what to do next. It's your choice, and, yes, you can choose to do nothing. Some will make that choice, because the problem is overwhelming and scary and hard and it feels like too much. But, you did read this whole book, so I really don't think you're a quitter. Remember, one step leads to the next and just like Earth has evolved, so will you. So when your frustration shifts to a need for action... Do you:

1. Decide this isn't about whose fault it is. Earth is home for all of us. We're in this together. By the end of today, you will do something. Anything. Maybe it's hanging your towels outside to dry, or donating some unneeded clothes, or walking somewhere instead of driving. All of those efforts add up to change when lots of people do them.

2. Choose to do more than one thing. Reflect on how you live and what changes you can make in the short and long term. (Please know that sometimes I do use a plastic straw and put my clothes (and towels) in the dryer, and while I'd love to have solar panels on my home, I don't yet. And you know what? It's okay. Because it's

a journey and doing something is better than doing nothing. Most likely, once you begin making changes to your lifestyle, you'll find yourself wanting to do more and more).

3. Think beyond what you can do. Talk to someone about what you've learned. Maybe it's a conversation with a parent, a teacher, a neighbor, or a friend. Maybe your conversation will lead to changes to your family's lifestyle, a new environmental club at school, or a community garden. Or maybe you'll inspire someone else to think about their own choices and realize how critical it is that we take action. The more we talk and share our ideas and support each other in change, the more it will feel like we truly are all in this together.

4. Consider a career in climate solutions. Maybe you can work in sustainable agriculture or research or engineering or environmental law. As our climate crisis increases, there will be more jobs and need for people in these solution-based fields. Like those mentioned in section two of this book, we need more Climate Change-makers!

5. Keep learning, keep asking the hard questions, and keep defending Earth's habitats and species. And, please, when you have the opportunity to do so, vote. If you're not happy with

the people on the ballot, consider running for office yourself and become a leader who leads us in the right direction.

*The title of this book has the word *may* in it for a reason. Things can be changed, or at the very least slowed, until we have more solutions. I believe it is your generation that needs to have the strongest voice in our future. Your values will shape new professions, policies, and most of all priorities. Your voice matters. Your choices matter. I believe we <u>will</u> survive, and it will be because of you.

Glossary

Glossary

acid	a sour substance with a pH level less than 7
acid rain	precipitation that is acidic, often due to sulfuric or nitric acid
advocate	a person who defends a cause
adaptation	evolutionary process of a species becoming better suited for survival in a habitat
agriculture	farming; the growing of crops or raising of animals for a profit
algae	single or multi-celled organisms that live in water or damp environments
alkalinity	a chemical measurement of water's ability to resist change in acid
anaerobic	existing without oxygen respiration
anatomy	the study of animal structure and parts
asteroid	a space rock that orbits our Sun
atmosphere	a series of layers of gas that surround Earth
Big Bang	the theory that an extremely dense point went through rapid expansion of matter, resulting in the Universe
biodiversity	also known as biological diversity; the wide variety of species found on Earth or in a habitat
biology	the study of life and the evolution of life

biomineralization	the process of living organisms producing minerals
BPA	Bisphenol-A, a chemical used to make and harden plastics
bycatch	unwanted organisms caught by the fishing industry
Cambrian explosion	between 541 and 530 million years ago, a great expanse of marine organisms and species marked the beginning of the Cambrian period
cap and trade	setting a limit on total use of resources or creation of pollution and allowing businesses to buy and trade within that limit
carbon dioxide	CO_2; a gas that's produced by burning fossil fuels
carbon footprint	the amount of greenhouse gas emissions that come from your choices and activities
carbon offsetting	funding efforts to reduce greenhouse emissions, such as planting trees, to balance out one's own greenhouse emissions
carbon tax	a fee based on the burning of fossil fuels to create products or for transportation
cataclysm	large-scale, catastrophic event
catastrophic	causing great damage
cellulose	molecular structure that forms the main structure of plants; found in the cell wall of plants
CFC	Chlorofluorocarbons: manufactured chemicals common in aerosol cans, food packaging, refrigerators, and air conditioners

changemaker	someone who takes action to solve problems
civilization	an advanced community
clean energy	also called renewable energy, energy with minimal greenhouse gas emissions
climate	the long-term average conditions produced by local or global weather patterns
climate change	long-term environmental changes caused by burning fossil fuels, which adds greenhouses gases to Earth's atmosphere
climate change-maker	someone who takes actions to help our current climate crisis
coal	a combustible rock made mostly of carbon; it's the remains of prehistoric plants and took millions of years to form
competition	an interaction between organisms, in which one is often harmed, as they pursue resources such as food and territory
compost	decayed organic material that becomes a fertilizer
consumer	one who purchases, eats, or uses something
continental drift	the theory that the continents are moving
convection currents	movement of magma in Earth's mantle that causes tectonic plates to move
cosmic dust	tiny particles of matter in space
crater	a bowl-shaped dent or hole in the ground
cross-pollination	the transfer of pollen from male reproductive organs from one plant to female reproductive organs of a different plant

crust	the outermost layer of rock on Earth; where humans live
cumulative effect	the combined impact of actions, positive or negative
DDT	dichlorodiphenyltrichloroethane, a pesticide used to kill insects that has been banned in over 30 countries
dead zones	an area of water that can't sustain life due to acid or the amount of dissolved oxygen
debris	scattered remains of broken down materials
decompose	break down or disintegrate
deforestation	the destruction or removal of forests through cutting or burning
density	a measure of the amount of mass compared to the volume; the denser the object, the heavier it will be
deposition	the process of soil, sediment, and rock building up, this often occurs after erosion and transportation of materials
disposable	made to be used only once or a few times
DNA	deoxyribonucleic acid; the genetic code for organisms that's in every cell and serves as an instruction manual for how organisms form
downcycling	recycling in which, the original material reduces in value or functionality in the next product that is made
drought	a long period of low or no rainfall

ecology	the study of organisms and their interactions in their habitat
element	substance that is so pure that it can't be broken down into other substances (examples are gold, iron, oxygen, helium)
emission	release out into the open
endangered species	a species at risk of extinction
entomologist	a person who studies insects
environmental racism	the systems in place that propel injustice through a disproportionate burden of intended or unintended environmental consequences and disadvantages on Black, Indigenous, and people of color
erosion	the process of soil, sediment, and rock being transported due to water, wind, ice, and gravity
equilibrium	a state of balance between opposing sides
espèces perdues	a French term that means lost species; extinct species
evolution	changes to a population over time occurring through natural selection
extinction	the death of a species, when no more individuals of that species exist
fast fashion	when clothes are created quickly and cheaply to follow current trends
feedback loop	a system; some is taken and some is returned; these can either be stable or unstable depending on how much is taken and how much is returned

forest fragmentation	the breaking apart of forests into separate pieces due to the building of roads, agriculture, and other human development
fossil fuel	coal, oil, or natural gas that comes from the remains of dead organisms
fossils	remains or imprints in rocks caused by an organism
fracking	or hydraulic fracturing; when the ground is drilled and a water solution is released into rock cracks, allowing access to fossil fuels
fungi	an organism that is not a plant or animal or bacteria that feeds on living matter; an agent of infectious disease
galaxy	a massive group of stars, planets, gas, dust, etc. that move together in space due to gravity
genes	coded instructions for how an organism develops
genetics	the study of genes
geology	the study of the earth; this includes Earth's structure, processes, natural resources, and fossils
gestation	the period when an animal is carried in the womb before birth
glaciation	when an area is covered by glaciers or ice sheets
greenhouse gases	gases that lead to Earth's surface and air warming
greenhouse effect	when the Sun's heat is trapped

gyres	a system of rotating currents in the ocean
habitat	the environment where species live
herbivore	an animal that eats plants
heredity	the process of passing on traits
hominin	primates from the zoological tribe Hominini; the only species existing in this tribe today are *Homo sapiens*
Homo sapiens	the scientific name for humans
humanitarian effort	an effort that relieves the suffering or pain of people
ice core	cylinders of ice that are drilled from glaciers or ice sheets; they hold particles from the atmosphere, which remain in the ice for thousands of years
incumbent	one that already occupies a position; a current politician running for office again is the incumbent
index fossil	a fossil that is useful in dating other fossils
indicator species	species, which include coral, frogs, and moss, that provide information about the overall health of an environment. These species are often the first impacted when an environment changes
Industrial Revolution	a period in the early 1800s, when factories cause widespread changes in manufacturing and transportation; more machines were used and less was made by hand
inner core	the innermost core of Earth

invasive species	a species that is not native and is causing economic/environmental harm
landfill	a place to dispose of waste
law of superposition	younger layers of rock are on top and the deeper down you go, the older the rocks get
leach	to drain; the movements of contaminants
legislation	laws, bills, and resolutions
leverage points	impact areas and opportunities toward a solution for a problem
litter	trash that is not thrown away correctly and is often found in nature
lobbyist	someone whose job it is to convince elected officials to vote in support of their cause or business
mammals	warm-blooded vertebrate animals, in which females produce milk and bear live young
mantle	Earth's layer between the outer core and crust
marine	sea; of the sea
mass extinction	a time in Earth's history when a large number of species go extinct over a short period
matter	anything that takes up space, which can be described by its state, such as liquid, solid, or gas
megafauna	large animals that weigh over a ton
meteor	an object from space that burns in Earth's atmosphere

meteorology	the study of weather and atmosphere
methane	a flammable gas that's a by-product of manure and decomposing organisms
microplastics	small pieces of plastic less than 5mm
migration	movement from one place to another
Milky Way	the galaxy that contains Earth, its solar system, and billions of other planets
natural gas	a gas, largely methane, extracted from Earth's crust
natural selection	the concept that organisms with favorable traits for survival are more likely to reproduce
nectar	a sweet liquid in flowers
New Pangaea	the concept that our continents are like one super-continent due to how quickly species are able to travel from one continent to another
nitrous oxide	a gas that comes from wastewater and is by-product of farming
nonrenewable resource	a natural resource that will eventually run out, like coal, gas, and natural gas
offspring	young born from an organism
organism	a living individual, such as a plant, animal, or single-celled life
outer core	a liquid rock layer surrounding Earth's inner core

ozone layer	one of the uppermost layers of Earth's atmosphere that blocks much of the sun's ultraviolet radiation
paleoanthropology	the study of human evolution
paleontology	the study of fossils
pandemic	a disease or virus that spreads over multiple continents or the entire world
Pangaea	the name for a supercontinent that formed around 335 million years ago and started breaking apart 175 million years ago
particle	a tiny bit of something
pesticides	chemicals used to prevent or kill unwanted organisms
pH	potential hydrogen is a measure of acidity or alkalinity, where 7 is neutral
photosynthesis	the process of plants making sunlight into sugar; plants use water, carbon dioxide, and sunlight to give off oxygen
plate tectonics	the concept that Earth is divided into plates that float over the mantle and move due to convection currents
policy	a course of action that guides decisions by the government, business, or organization
pollinators	animals that moves pollen from the male part of the flower (anther) to the female part (stigma) of another flower leading to pollination
pollination	the transfer of pollen from flower to flower to create offspring

pollution	harmful contamination of the environment
prey	an animal that is killed for food
primates	any member of the biological order Primates, this includes lemurs, apes, humans, etc.
profit over people	when businesses and money are put before the best interest of people (Noam Chomsky wrote a famous book with this title)
profit over planet	when money is put before the best interest of the planet and the species living on it
radiometric dating	determining the age of a geological material by examining the presence of radioactive elements
recycle	reusing part or all of something that would be waste
renewable resource	a natural resource that doesn't run out, like solar energy
reproduction	the process of organisms producing offspring
salinity	containing salt; the concentration of salt to water
selective breeding	also called artificial selection; breeding to get desired characteristics
slickwater	or slick water; a water solution with acids and sand or clay that's used in fracking
solar energy	when the sun's energy is captured by solar panels' solar cells and turned into electrical energy
solar panels	a panel with solar cells that absorb the sun's rays and convert light into electrical energy

solar system	a group of celestial bodies that orbit around a star
species	a group of living organism that are similar and can interbreed
stakeholders	those with an interest in the outcome of a problem or situation
subsidies	benefits given to an individual or group, often involving removal of something like taxes or fees
sustainable	able to be maintained; on-going
tax	money that is paid to the government
taxonomy	the naming and classifying of organisms into groups
tax rebate	a refund of money from the government for overpaying taxes or as an incentive to take certain actions
tax subsidies	a reduction in taxes to reduce the cost of something
tectonic plates	massive slabs of rock that floats on Earth's mantle; they can be thousands of miles across
terrestrial	land; of the earth
threatened species	a species likely to become endangered
tipping point	a critical point of change
trait	characteristics of an organism that come from genes
trilobites	a species that mainly lived in shallow water and existed for 270 million years; an important index fossil today

uniformitarianism	also called the doctrine of uniformity, states that Earth's processes act in the same manner today as they did in the past
universe	Everything; all planets, stars, gas, dust, organisms
vector	an organism that carries and transmits something infectious to another organism or population of organisms
vertebrate	an animal with a backbone
virus	an agent of infectious disease; a microscopic parasite that infects living organisms
water cycle	the cycle of water moving through Earth's ocean, freshwater, land, plants, animals and sky
wind energy	energy created when wind turbines convert the wind into electricity

To Further Your Understanding

The following books and documentaries can help enhance understanding of Earth, evolution, *Homo sapiens*, and our current climate crisis.

<u>Recommended Reading</u>

The Story of Earth: The First 4.5 Billion Years, from Stardust to Living Planet by Robert M. Hazen
- A sequential overview of Earth's history.

The Sixth Extinction: An Unnatural History by Elizabeth Kolbert
- Evidence from the past and present that we're currently living in a mass extinction event.

Climate Change: What Everyone Needs To Know by Joseph Romm
- An overview of the science behind climate change, evidence, and policy.

Evolution: The Triumph of an Idea by Carl Zimmer
- An overview of evolution and how it impacts us today.

Reading the Rocks: The Autobiography of Earth by Marcia Bjornerud
- Background information on geological concepts and Earth's history.

The Story of the Earth in 25 Rocks: Tales of Important Geological Puzzles and the People Who Solved Them by Donald R. Prothero
- Rocks and the people who made discoveries that shaped our current understanding of geology and Earth's history.

T. rex and the Crater of Doom by Walter Alvarez
- How the theory arose that an asteroid caused a mass extinction event that killed the dinosaurs; written by one of the scientists who made the discovery.

Recommended Viewing

An Inconvenient Truth directed by Davis Guggenheim
  - A landmark documentary that reveals evidence of climate change and the impact it will have.

Before the Flood directed by Fisher Stevens
  - An overview of the catastrophic impacts that people face due to climate change.

Earth: Making of a Planet directed by Yavar Abbas
  - A computer animated overview of Earth's history.

I Am Greta directed by Nathan Grossman
  - This documentary follows Greta Thunberg over two years of her life, including her speaking at the UN Climate Action Summit in 2019.

Our Planet directed by Sophie Lanfear
  - A documentary series that leaves you in awe of Earth's varying ecosystems and species.

The Day the Mesozoic Died directed by Sarah Holt
  - An overview of the theory that an asteroid killed the dinosaurs and led to a mass extinction event.

Who Killed the Electric Car? directed by Chris Paine
  - The story of Electric Vehicle 1 (EV1) shows how policy, lobbyists, and industries are shaping what products are available to consumers.

2040 directed by Damon Gameau
  - A prediction of what Earth will be like in 20 years, mixed with optimism for what we can do to find solutions.

Acknowledgements

Thank you to Penny Noyce at Tumblehome Books for her editing feedback and believing in this project. This is my fourth book with Penny as my editor and she has the amazing balance of helping my writing develop in terms of form and function, and showing the utmost support. Thank you to Yu-Yi Ling for her layout and design, and her endless patience with my creative visions.

Thank you to Chris Schadler who taught "Contemporary Issues in Environmental Conservation," which I took in the fall semester of my freshman year of college. Her teaching style, passion, and the topics she covered lit a fire in me, which led me to focus my studies around environmental science, psychology, and education.

Thank you to Elizabeth Kolbert, who is the author of *The Sixth Extinction: An Unnatural History*. Her book is packed with evidence and anecdotes that left me feeling empowered to do something with all that she taught me. A few years ago, I reached out to her via email and amazingly she wrote back. Unknowingly, her words gave me the courage to write this book and find my own voice that interweaves my knowledge with my 20 years of experience as an educator.

A huge thank you to my beta readers, Andrew McCullough, Sarah Dawson, Eli Wilson, and Greta Holmes, who gave valuable feedback and insight on the manuscript. And last, but by no means least, a huge thank you to my students. You inspire me each day and give me hope for what the future holds. You make me believe that we *will* change the path we're on, and not only survive, but become a more creative-thinking and compassionate species.

About the Author

Katie Coppens is an award winning middle school science  teacher with her Masters in Teaching with a concentration in environmental science. She's been a classroom teacher for 20 years, with a range of experiences, including teaching high school English and biology in Tanzania. Katie's a columnist for the National Science Teaching Association's Science Scope magazine on the topic of integrating science and literacy. She also authored NSTA's *Creative Writing in Science: Activities that Inspire.* Katie's children's books include: The Acadia Files chapter book series, *Geology is a Piece of Cake*, and *Geometry is as Easy as Pie*. She is the co-author of *What Do Black Holes Eat For Dinner? And Other Silly, Yet Totally Smart, Questions About Space.* Please visit www.katiecoppens.com for more information on her publications.

The purpose of this book is to educate and empower, with no agenda of personal profit. Therefore, all author pay and royalties from this book are being donated to the non-profit organization *One Tree Planted*, which plants trees to help global reforestation. Please go to https://onetreeplanted.org/ to learn more about the local and global impacts of this organization. Tumblehome Books is a nonprofit publishing company whose mission is to inspire young people in science through the power of story.

Sources

The following books were the main sources for this book and have served as my foundation of knowledge around the topics of Earth's history, evolution, mass extinctions, and climate change:

Alvarez, Walter. *T. Rex and the Crater of Doom*. Princeton University Press, 2008.

Bjornerud, Marcia. *Reading the Rocks: the Autobiography of the Earth*. BasicBooks, 2007.

Hazen, Robert M. *The Story of Earth: The First 4.5 Billion Years, from Stardust to Living Planet*. Penguin Books. 2013.

Kolbert, Elizabeth. *The Sixth Extinction: An Unnatural History*. Bloomsbury, 2015.

Prothero, Donald R. *The Story of the Earth in 25 Rocks*. Columbia University Press, 2018.

Romm, Joseph J. *Climate Change: What Everyone Needs to Know*. Oxford University Press, 2018.

Zimmer, Carl. *Evolution: the Triumph of an Idea*. William Heinemann, 2001.

Over 250 additional text, video, and web sources were used in the writing of this book. Go to the publisher's website, https://tumblehome-books.org/earthwillsurvive, to view sources organized by chapter.

Photo Credits

Images included in this book are public domain, photos by the author, provided by the Climate Change-makers, or found on Creative Commons/Wikipedia:Images/Unsplash with appropriate credit given below. Image use should not be considered an endorsement of the book.

FRONT COVER
Butterfly- Rhododendrites
https://commons.wikimedia.org/wiki/File:Monarch_butterfly_in_BBG_(84685).jpg

Girl- Happiness Stephen
https://commons.wikimedia.org/wiki/File:African-haya_girl.jpg

Galapagos Penguin- Mike's Birds
https://commons.wikimedia.org/wiki/File:Galapagos_Penguin_(46860487615).jpg

Common Snail- macrophile
https://commons.wikimedia.org/wiki/File:Common_snail.jpg

Woman- Happiness Stephen
https://commons.wikimedia.org/wiki/File:African-haya_girl.jpg

Rhino- Alvinategyeka
https://commons.wikimedia.org/wiki/File:Ziwa_rhino_sanctuary.jpg

Reef Fish- incidencematrix
https://commons.wikimedia.org/wiki/File:Reef_Fish_(23563499860).jpg

Bubmlebee- Martin Falbisoner
https://commons.wikimedia.org/wiki/File:Bumblebee_on_Lavender_Blossom.JPG

Baby Sea turtle- Wildlifeppl
https://commons.wikimedia.org/wiki/File:Baby_Sea_Turtle.jpg

Moose- Magnus Manske
https://commons.wikimedia.org/wiki/File:Moose_in_Grand_Teton_National_Park_3_(8007698498).jpg

Eurasian tree sparrow- Peter P. Othagoer
https://commons.wikimedia.org/wiki/File:Passer_montanus_malaccensis_@_

Kuala_Lumpur,_Malaysia_(1).jpg

Koala- Till Niermann
https://commons.wikimedia.org/wiki/File:Koala_in_Zoo_Duisburg.jpg

Crab- John Dickens
https://commons.wikimedia.org/wiki/File:Horneyed-ghost-crab-24403401.jpg

Ant- Bulldog Pottery - Bruce Gholson and Samantha Henne Use this instead of ant on original cover
https://search.creativecommons.org/photos/26886703-127e-495b-a7bb-8-c5bd7870197

Giraffe- Mike Setchell
https://unsplash.com/photos/pf97TYdQlWM

Tiger- andibreit
https://pixabay.com/photos/tiger-swamp-big-cat-wild-cat-2535888/

TITLE PAGE
The Blue Marble by the crew of Apollo 17- NASA/Apollo 17 crew; taken by either Harrison Schmitt or Ron Evans
https://en.wikipedia.org/wiki/The_Blue_Marble#/media/File:The_Earth_seen_from_Apollo_17.jpg

CHAPTER 1
A dinosaur femur- James St. John
https://commons.wikimedia.org/wiki/File:Diplodocus_sp._(sauropod_dinosaur_femur)_(Morrison_Formation,_Upper_Jurassic;_Carnegie_Quarry,_Dinosaur_National_Monument,_Utah,_USA)_2_(48696480548).jpg

Sauropod dinosaur remains- Einar Fredriksen
https://commons.wikimedia.org/wiki/File:Sauropods.jpg

Mastodon remains- Bill Abbott
https://commons.wikimedia.org/wiki/File:Mastadon_DSC_2009_(23255615833).jpg

Mary Anning- Mr. Grey' in Crispin Tickell's book 'Mary Anning of Lyme Regis' (1996)
https://commons.wikimedia.org/wiki/File:Mary_Anning_painting.jpg

Mary Anning' Plesiosaur - Txllxt TxllxT (cropped from original image)
https://commons.wikimedia.org/wiki/File:London_-_Cromwell_Road_-_

Photo Credits

Natural_History_Museum_1881_by_Alfred_Waterhouse_-_Mary_Anning,_the_Fossil_Woman.jpg

CHAPTER 2
Representations of *Homo sapiens*
https://commons.wikimedia.org/wiki/File:Homo_sapiens_-_Paleolithic_-_reconstruction-_MUSE.jpg- Matteo De Stefano/MUSE
https://commons.wikimedia.org/wiki/File:Homo_sapiens_-_Mesolithic_-_reconstruction-_MUSE.jpg- Matteo De Stefano/MUSE
https://commons.wikimedia.org/wiki/File:Homo_sapiens_-_Neolithic_-_reconstruction_-_MUSE.jpg- Matteo De Stefano/MUSE
https://unsplash.com/photos/KGN-oA5h6BA- Christian Bowen
https://unsplash.com/photos/6qfxmy3657c- Alice Muriithi
https://unsplash.com/photos/vpwDZgKtgVk- Alex Robinson

A chimpanzee- Dkoukoul (cropped from original image)
https://commons.wikimedia.org/wiki/File:Chimpanzee_Attica_Zoological_Park_2.jpg

CHAPTER 3
Alfred Wegener (cropped)- public domain in the USA.
https://commons.wikimedia.org/wiki/File:Wegener_Expedition-1930_026.jpg

Marie Tharp and Bruce Heezen- marie tharp maps
https://www.flickr.com/photos/marietharpmaps/537480113/

Helen Vaughn Michel, Frank Asaro, Walter Alvarez, and Luis Alvarez- permission from Berkeley Lab photography archive

Greta Thunberg- Anders Hellberg
https://commons.wikimedia.org/wiki/File:Greta_Thunberg_4.jpg

CHAPTER 4
CREDO Action & New Yorkers Against Fracking Protest Gov. Cuomo's Plan to Frack New York" by CREDO: Cuomo Policy Summit
https://search.creativecommons.org/photos/1598399f-51d8-4ac8-970f-f5702d722188

A nuclear power plant's cooling towers- Roberto Uderio.
https://commons.wikimedia.org/wiki/File:Cofrentes_nuclear_power_plant_cooling_towers_retouched.jpg

Data of Earth's average temperature over time (in °C)
RCraig09, CC BY-SA 4.0 <https://creativecommons.org/licenses/by-sa/4.0>,

via Wikimedia Commons

Polar bears are a threatened species under the Endangered Species Act-AWeith
https://commons.wikimedia.org/wiki/File:Polar_bear_(Ursus)_maritimus_female_with_its_cub,_Svalbard_(2).jpg

The Republic of Maldives- nattu
https://search.creativecommons.org/photos/d43bbcaf-1ba0-4c41-a42a-948-bab0b47f2

Marina Silva- Marina Silva

Nick Paul- USC Seaweed Research Group

CHAPTER 5
The arctic- Brocken Inaglory
https://commons.wikimedia.org/wiki/File:Icebergs_in_the_High_Arctic_-_20050907.jpg

The rainforest- Shao
https://commons.wikimedia.org/wiki/File:Amazonian_rainforest_2.JPG
Healthy coral- Great Barrier Reef Encounter

Healthy coral- Great Barrier Reef Encounter
https://commons.wikimedia.org/wiki/File:Snorkeling_on_the_Great_Barrier_Reef.jpg

Trees being planted in Seychelles- Patrick Joubert
https://commons.wikimedia.org/wiki/File:Planting_a_tree_on_the_compound_of_La_Digue_school.jpg

Deforestation in New Zealand- Martin Wegmann
https://commons.wikimedia.org/wiki/File:Deforestation_NZ_TasmanWestCoast_3_MWegmann.jpg

Wangari Maathai
https://commons.wikimedia.org/wiki/File:Wangari_Maathai_in_2001.jpg

CHAPTER 6
Neanderthal representation- Neanderthal-Museum, Mettmann
https://commons.wikimedia.org/wiki/File:Homo_sapiens_neanderthalensis-Mr._N.jpg

Diprotodon- Emőke Dénes
https://commons.wikimedia.org/wiki/File:Em_-_Diprotodon_optatum_-_4.jpg

Moa reconstruction- Archives New Zealand
https://commons.wikimedia.org/wiki/File:Hunting_the_Moa.jpg

Megatherium- Biodiversity Heritage Library
https://upload.wikimedia.org/wikipedia/commons/a/a2/Skeleton_of_Megatherium.jpg

An African bush elephant- Muhammad Mahdi Karim
https://commons.wikimedia.org/wiki/File:African_Bush_Elephant.jpg

IUCN's Red List- Peter Halasz. (User:Pengo)
https://commons.wikimedia.org/wiki/File:Status_iucn2.3.svg

Sofia Molina- Marco Molina

CHAPTER 7
A gecko from Borneo- Firos AK
https://commons.wikimedia.org/wiki/File:Asian_House_Gecko_close_up_from_bangalore.jpg

Mono Lake- King of Hearts
https://commons.wikimedia.org/wiki/File:Mono_Lake_South_Tufa_August_2013_012.jpg

Plastic being sorted- Kirti Nagar
https://unsplash.com/photos/-4bD2p5zbdA

Ocean plastic and trash- Kevin Krejci
https://commons.wikimedia.org/wiki/File:Plastic_Ocean_(4408273247).jpg

Microplastics- Clandon haverford
https://commons.wikimedia.org/wiki/File:Microplastic_sample.jpg

Art exhibit plastic bags/jellyfish-photo by U+1F360 (art by Washed Ashore at Mote Marine Aquarium)
https://commons.wikimedia.org/wiki/File:Plastic_Bag_Jelly_Fish.jpg

Laura Marston- Searching the Shadows Photography

CHAPTER 8
Nile Perch- Daiju Azuma
https://en.wikipedia.org/wiki/Nile_perch#/media/File:Lates_niloticus_by_
DaijuAzuma.jpg

Green crab- Andrew McCullough

Common snapping turtle- Dakota L.
https://en.wikipedia.org/wiki/Common_snapping_turtle#/media/
File:Common_Snapping_Turtle_Close_Up.jpg

Asian hornet- Gilles San Martin
https://commons.wikimedia.org/wiki/File:Asian_hornet_(33252984804)_(2).
jpg

CHAPTER 9
U.S. Capitol Building- Louis Velazquez
https://unsplash.com/photos/XWW746i6WoM

Campaign signs- Michael Carruth
https://unsplash.com/photos/VoYhILXi64o

Fossil Fuel subsidies- Climate crisis rally Melbourne by John Englart (Takver)
https://search.creativecommons.org/photos/9be74b41-686a-48b4-88af-6-
b3e9098a96e

Xiuhtezcatl Martinez- Josué Rivas
https://commons.wikimedia.org/wiki/File:Xiuhtezcatl_Martinez_for_Stand-
ing_Strong_Project_(cropped).jpg

Hindou Oumarou Ibrahim- Fatakaya
https://commons.wikimedia.org/wiki/File:Hindou_Oumarou_Ibrahim.jpg

CHAPTER 10
Australian wildfires- Meganesia
https://commons.wikimedia.org/wiki/File:Gospers_Mountain_Fire.jpg

https://www.worldometers.info/coronavirus/country/us/

SARS-CoV-2- Felipe Esquivel Reed
https://commons.wikimedia.org/wiki/File:Coronavirus_SARS-CoV-2.jpg

Michael Jarvis- jarvislab.com

CHAPTER 11
Clothing being made- Rio Lecatompessy
https://unsplash.com/photos/cfDURuQKABk

A yard sale- Donatella D'Anniballe
https://unsplash.com/photos/1Q6qGGBduY4

CHAPTER 12
Greenhouse gas contributions of an average diet- (recreated) Center for Sustainable Systems, University of Michigan. 2020. "Carbon Footprint Factsheet." Pub. No. CSS09-05. http://css.umich.edu/factsheets/carbon-footprint-factsheet

Pounds of CO_2 per serving- (recreated) Center for Sustainable Systems, University of Michigan. 2020. "Carbon Footprint Factsheet." Pub. No. CSS09-05. http://css.umich.edu/factsheets/carbon-footprint-factsheet

Bananas after harvest- Henry Doe
https://unsplash.com/photos/85Cv18FAvEk

A farmer's market- Gary Butterfield
https://unsplash.com/photos/E7Jt6s6EuOs

Bee- Amy Lynn Grover
https://unsplash.com/photos/Nh8Mx1RDZ2k

CHAPTER 13
A pile of junk mail- Dvortygirl
https://commons.wikimedia.org/wiki/File:Pile_of_junk_mail.jpg

CHAPTER 14
Towels hung out to dry- Annie Spratt
https://unsplash.com/photos/ehX9bG8Inc4

CHAPTER 15
I voted sticker- Steve Rainwater (cropped)
https://commons.wikimedia.org/wiki/File:I_voted_today_2018-02-25_06-42-43_-_38676565790.jpg

Voting in the 2016 presidential election
https://ourworldindata.org/usa-electoral-turnout